SWEDISH TRADITIONS

Jan-Öjvind Swahn

SWEDISH TRADITIONS

Translation: Rachelle Puryear

ORDALAGET BOKFÖRLAG

IN SEVERAL LANGUAGES!

GERMAN

SPANISH

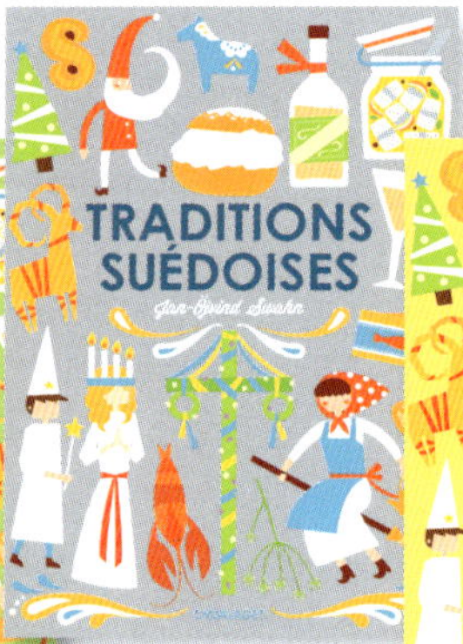

FRENCH

SWEDISH

IMAGE RESEARCH, TYPOGRAPHY AND
GRAFIC DESIGN: Helena Jansson Icardo, Margot Henrikson, Mattias Henrikson
TEXT EDITOR: Anna Nolgren
COVER DESIGN: Elena Lombardi

Ordalaget Bokförlag AB
Box 17018
167 17 Bromma
bok@ordalaget.se

Visit our website: www.ordalaget.se

PICTURES: **Mattias Henrikson** pages 14, 23, 27, 62, 64, 65, 70, 80–81, 84–85, 86, 87, 106, 120, 140–141, 143; **Scanpix** pages 48 (Lars Ottosson), 61 (Henrik Montgomery), 74 (Leif Jacobsson), 88 (Gunnar Lundmark), 150 (Janerik Henriksson); **Ulrika Pousette** pages 108, 114, 126–127, 138; **Majblommans Riksförbund** page 44–45; **Nordiska museet** pages 38, 58; **Nationalmuseum** pages 67, 76–77; Bertil Lybeck/**BUS** 2012 page 95; **Helena Jansson Icardo** page 109; **Carl Larsson-gården**, Sundborn page 116; Jenny Nyström/**BUS** 2012 page 122–123.

Printing: Livonia print, Latvia, 2022
ISBN: 978-91-7469-040-8

Content

Introduction

Discussions about how people lived in the old days are usually illustrated with very gloomy images and descriptions of how awful things were. When someone tries to compound all of this wretchedness by adding to it the fact that our forefathers did not even have vacations, then I cannot refrain from correcting this flawed notion of past society. The truth is that people actually had just as much leisure time as we do, even though there was only one week of vacation stipulated by law.

Religious Holidays and Work-related Celebrations

Midsummer brings to an end the half of the year which, beginning with Advent, is so richly endowed with religious holidays. On the other hand, the following six months are quite lacking in such traditions even today. This is undoubtedly a result of summers and autumns being particularly full of the long and arduous labor performed by the self-sufficient country folks who made up the majority of the population in Sweden long ago. There was haymaking and harvest, threshing and slaughtering, preparing flax and weaving, churning butter and making cheese, bread and beer. So there just was not enough time left to celebrate any holidays. Of course this did not mean that summer and autumn lacked festive occasions. These were not regulated by the religious calendar but rather by the *Farmer's Almanac:* haymaking celebrations and harvest porridge, cheesemaking festivals and dung dances.

New Holidays and Extended Weekends (Klämdagar)

During our times, the two recently established red letter holidays on the Swedish calendar, namely May Day on May 1 and our National Holiday on June 6, belong to a new category of holidays called civil holidays, a term inspired by other non-religious phenomena that occur during our life cycles: civil confirmations, civil weddings, and civil funerals. However it has proven difficult to create more universally widespread traditions in connection with these dates. Moreover, when our National Day was just an ordinary working day it was very difficult to instill it with the same kind of intensity accorded Norway's Constitution Day on May 17. May 1 is quite a different matter; it harks back to medieval times as a civil holiday – today's day of dwindling demonstrations did not appear until the end of the 19th century.

The popular Swedish notion of a *klämdag* connotes a day which becomes a holiday because it falls on the day before or after a holiday. What creates a klämdag (literally a "squeezed day") is of course those holidays which do not include a weekend. Easter and Pentecost have no such days, while Ascension Thursday affects the next day so that Thursday and Friday together automatically create a four day weekend because of the Friday "squeezed in between." This produces a wonderful extended spring holiday which begins for many people already at noon on Wednesday. At best (from a working perspective), the Christmas holidays can generate so many of these days which fall between holidays that the possibility arises of having a Christmas break that can be several weeks long if one is willing to forgo a few vacation days here or there. Naturally, different factions of the labor market soon made agreements which allowed people to make up for lost work hours in advance. In addition one might even have such a bad headache or tummy ache during the Christmas holidays that the need to take a few days of sick leave would arise at some point during this extended vacation.

Shrove Tuesday Buns

Fettisdagen

One Tuesday
Febr 3–March 9

During a visit to Visby on the island of Gotland I met a pastry chef who emphatically declared that it was in this town that the modern Shrove Tuesday Bun (*semla*) with its whipped cream collar saw the light of day. Its inventor, the master baker Henrik Reinhold Pettersson, supposedly was inspired by whipping cream once again becoming available after the end of World War I. This to a population who had been craving cream and who thus were able to finally have their fill, even though the season for the bun back then was strictly limited to the weeks of Lent. I cannot vouch for the veracity of this attribution, but it will have to do for the time being.

A Beloved Child Has Many Names

The beloved Shrove Tuesday buns have many different names in Swedish: *semlor*, Lenten buns (*fastlagsbullar*), Fat Tuesday buns (*fettisdagsbullar*), or *hetvägg* when served in a bowl of warm milk. The oldest name is *hetvägg*, (first noted in Sweden in 1689) which is a barely understandable translation of the German *heisse Wecken*, meaning warm wedges or buns. *Semla* (plural, *semlor*) is the name it has long been known by in the vicinity of Stockholm. Semla, and the name *hetvägg* which were

The modern Shrove Tuesday Bun (semla), a "warm bun with whipped cream and milk", became popular in the mid-20th century.

both borrowed from Low German, meant bread made from finely sifted wheat flour. No matter what it was named before, it was primarily a treat enjoyed by city folk, especially the bourgeoisie. In Stockholm they could be bought readymade in bakeries 200 years ago, although they most often were made at home. Since the joint advertising campaigns of the bakeries and pastry shops for this important economic product originate in our Royal Capital, they all use the Stockholm term *semla*, and unfortunately it is only a matter of time before the other names will disappear. In addition, the name *semla* has the advantage of having absolutely no connection to Lent or fasting, so that they can start selling them already after the Epiphany without even blushing. (Yes, I have seen semlor in pastry shop windows even before Christmas!) Traditionally the buns were made by scooping out the center of the bun and mixing the insides with cream, butter and almonds and stuffing the mixture back into the bun. From the mid-1800s the process was simplified by using almond paste to replace the mixture.

Whipped cream is the latest addition to the modern semla, and this has transformed it into something of a calorie bomb. When this became common, the practice of eating the bun with warm milk and cinnamon disappeared – milk does not go well with whipped cream. Nowadays the bun is mainly considered to be a seasonal pastry for coffee breaks and lunch.

Flirting Buns

The prehistory of the *semla* also involves a system of flirting in southern Sweden. The farmhands would give the maids Lenten buns during the Lent parties that were customary in the villages. During the 19th century they were often saffron flavored wheat buns with a few raisins inside. The girl who was given a bun was supposed to return the favor by giving the donor a number of eggs for Easter. Thus *semlor* often wove marital bands.

On one occasion the tradition of these hot buns dripping with fat caused the sudden demise of a Swedish king. This was the fate of the Swedish king Adolf Fredrik, the father of Gustav III, whose last meal, eaten on Shrove Tuesday in 1771, consisted of "*hetvägg*, sauerkraut, meat and turnips, lobster, caviar and champagne," according to the diary of Count J. G. Oxenstierna. The king died of overeating after consuming this bizarre meal. A priest's death, according to the court, although there certainly are worse ways of dying.

The Shrove Tuesday Bun (semla) was already in existence in Sweden during the 13th century – however it did not contain whipped cream. It might have looked something like this on Shrove Tuesday morning about a century ago. The illustration is by Elsa Beskow, one of Sweden's most beloved illustrators of children's books, 1909.

Waffle Day

Våffeldagen

March 25

This holiday was considered to be the introduction to spring or even to summer in southern Sweden. In many places the name of the day was Our Lady's Day, or *Vårfrudagen* in Swedish, which naturally gave rise to associations to spring. Weather predictions generally provided tips as to how long it would be before spring arrived. A good sign of spring was when a child could walk all the way around the outside of the cottage without stepping in snow.

Did you know that in many countries – and even sporadically in the Nordic countries – the Annunciation, or *Marie bebådelsedag* as it is called in Swedish, was considered to be New Year's Day, at least during the Middle Ages? This was actually the case in England up until 1752. So now you know!

The Swedish name of the day, *Vårfrudagen* (Our Lady's Day) was mispronounced in many Swedish dialects. In the parts of Sweden where the consonants L and R are pronounced with a retroflex flap, people gradually altered the pronunciation to *Vafferdagen*, and later on to *Vaffeldagen*. Since the Swedish word *vaffla* was an antiquated form of the Swedish word for a waffle, *våffla*, a permanent association to this particular food was established.

"Crispy waffles made with Mamma's waffle iron from Husqvarna," an advertisement from the 1940s.

The First of April

Första april

Ever since the 16th century people have played practical jokes in countries like Germany, where jokes on April Fools' Day were very popular among all of the social classes. However the custom could also be found in England, France, Portugal, Spain and elsewhere. Outside of Europe we find that the ancient Persians certainly had no April, yet they played jokes on each other on approximately the same day that we do. There must be something in the air around this time of year. Hindus had the same practice.

There are a great number of suggestions as to which historical events could be the reason for the origin of this custom, but they all seem just as implausible. The fact is that we do not know their origin and we probably never will.

April Fools' Jokes – The Nordic Way

April Fools' pranks first appeared in Sweden during the 1670s. In 1742 the first real April Fools' joke that we actually know about in Sweden was staged – a prankster nailed a notice up on the door of the church in Hällstad in the province of Västergötland which announced that the next high mass would be held

Like an April Fools' joke, the first coltsfoot flower appears in glowing yellow in April.

one hour earlier than usual, whereby "great commotion arose among a crowd of the parishioners, who thereby had been tricked," as was written in a disapproving record of the proceedings of the parish council.

April, April, You Silly Herring!

There has also been found a more popular parallel, though it is not associated with any particular date on the calendar, but rather refers to the end of an extensive period of farm labor or the end of a particular training program. For example, when fertilization was finished, a newly employed farmhand could be sent to a neighbor in order to borrow the butt drill.

I spent summers as a young boy on an island in the archipelago, and one day I heard that they were going to slaughter a pig on a neighboring farm. I had never seen anyone die, least of all a pig, so I rushed over there to look. Right when they came leading the sacrificial victim squealing like a pig who knows that its days are numbered, the farmer turned to his wife and said: "Where is the thingamajig?" She answered, "Goodness, I lent it out to the Nilssons!"

Everyone looked at me and someone said: "Listen, run over to the Nilssons right away and ask them to give you back our thingamajig, otherwise we won't be able to slaughter the pig!" I ran off, happy to play a role in the pig's departure from this earthly life. The Nilssons were in on the game and said they were sorry but that they had lent it to the Karlssons. I ran from farm to farm until I realized that a thingamajig was nothing real, and when I sullenly returned to the barnyard the pig was already dead and butchered.

This was the kind of popular practical jokes that refined people usually connected to the first of April long ago. It was exactly this type of April Fools' prank, sending people on errands where they ended up being fooled into going somewhere for no good reason, which were standard jokes both on the continent and in the Nordic countries up until the time when newspapers began reporting prankster news during the last century. But why is the person being fooled compared to a herring in the classic Swedish rhyme that is recited after pulling a prank: "*April, april, din dumma sill, dej kan jag lura vart jag vill!*" (April, April, you silly herring, I can fool you into going anywhere!)? Of course the intelligent reader says that it is because it rhymes in Swedish, but that is certainly not the answer! Because the fish is often a herring, even in languages where the name of the fish does not rhyme with April at all: it is *Hering* in German, *Poisson d'avril* in French, etc. Herring actually have an old reputation of not being very smart, perhaps because they let themselves be caught so easily.

On April 1, 1950 the Swedish newspaper *Göteborgs-Posten* candidly reported that the island of Öland, having loosened from its foundations, was moving westward and would soon become a part of the province of Småland.

A classic example of an April Fools' prank is the one from 1960, the time before Sweden had color TV, where the famous radio and TV reporter Kjell Stensson began a very serious demonstration of how to transform a black and white TV into a modern color TV set. He cut a nylon stocking and taped it over the TV screen and abracadabra, it was transformed into a color TV. That program clip supposedly resulted in the ruin of a good number of nylon stockings.

Palm Sunday

Palmsöndagen

According to Chapter 12 in the gospel of St. John, the last Sunday before Easter, Palm Sunday, got its name from the palm fronds which people broke off and strewed in front of Jesus in order to pay tribute to him as he entered Jerusalem on a donkey. For a very long time these palms would play an important role in the start of the Easter celebration. However because there is a scarcity of palm trees north of the Alps, it was necessary to come up with a substitute. In Germany they used all kinds of evergreens such as ivy or even budding branches of sallow or willow trees. The latter was the only choice available in Scandinavia.

All Sorts of Magic Palms

The artificial palms in central Europe had the most spectacular designs, where they developed into something much like small May poles with flowers. They were brought to church where the priest would bless them. We know that there were also customs like these in Sweden during the Middle Ages.

It is very reasonable to wonder whether our birch branches decorated with colorful feathers (*påskris*) or Lent switches (*fastlagsris*), the branches which were used to give whippings (see the chapter on Easter), could be related to the impressive continental palms. Very often there were colored hollow eggs hanging from the birch branches in the olden days. That these decorated branches first appeared in the Stockholm area may be an indication that in the beginning they were a substitute for the more resplendent artificial palms that the many Germans in the capital city were used to back home.

Easter

Påsk

Easter is the one celebration which most markedly couples together Christianity and Judaism. The Easter Passion is so linked to Jewish culture that to this day it still follows the Jewish lunar calendar which allowed the crucifixion to become a part of the annual Passover celebration, *Pesach*, in Jerusalem about the year 33 A. D.

The Swedish word for Easter, *påsk,* is an adaption of the Hebrew word *pesach*, which was the pre-Hebraic name of a shepherds' feast as well as its main dish: Easter lamb.

Mortification in the Past, Entertainment Today

For the majority of Swedish people whose interest in religion can be considered to be tepid, Easter has primarily become a four day work free holiday which, at least in southern and central Sweden, can fall at a point in time which is perfect for spring cleaning of gardens, getting sailboats ready for the summer or making the first visit of the year to one's summer cottage. Yet Easter is a moveable feast, and if it happens to fall already in March then in the northernmost parts of Sweden it usually offers the opportunity for winter sports rather than outdoor chores. The gardeners wishing to produce the countless yellow daffodils, which have become the main Easter decorations in our homes often in combination with birch

Yellow, the color of the daffodils in the picture, is the Easter color, as we all know. The yellow color harks back to the role that eggs and chickens came to play at Easter. All of the eggs which had been stored during Lent had to be eaten when Lent finally ended on Easter Day.

branches, are among those who have the most problems with the changeable placement of Easter on the calendar. As we all know, yellow is the Easter color, and this goes back to the role that eggs and chickens came to play at Easter – although yellow is not the church's liturgical color for Easter.

The first generation of Lutheran priests tried to get their parishioners to stop many of the numerous customs that were a part of the Catholic tradition. This included fasting among other things, and many people wanted to show their religious zealousness by gorging on pork during Lent. The pendulum swung back, and several generations ago Good Friday was marked by mortification in most homes. People would often eat salted foods such as salt herring or dried cod, salted cheese or flavorless flour porridge. The resulting thirst was not supposed to be quenched in order to experience the same thirst Christ had on the cross. Under no circumstances was one supposed to drink milk or cream – I have met people who even today will not put cream in their coffee on Good Friday.

There were also other ways of trying to create an atmosphere that was as sorrowful as possible. It was not until the 1970s that movie theaters were allowed to show any films other than different versions of the Passion of Christ.

Even today a variety of fish dishes are usual Good Friday fare. This is reminiscent of the fact that in some areas this day was observed as a day of fasting – and thereby a fish day – for a very long time after the Reformation. However nowadays delicacies such as poached or smoked salmon are served, in both cases with sauces which definitely do not meet the fasting restrictions.

Witch Feasts and Easter Kisses

On Holy Thursday, Easter hags (påskkärringar) and witches knock on doors asking for coins or some candy in their coffee pots.

At least in protestant countries Holy Saturday, the day before Easter, has become just the opposite of Good Friday. This is the day when most families stuff themselves with eggs – with or without the assistance of the Easter Bunny, even though they really should wait until Easter Sunday!

Today an eerie, ancient feature of the Swedish Easter celebration has been transformed into a kind of entertainment for children. Children dressed in kerchiefs and long skirts walk the streets carrying old fashioned coffee kettles which they expect to have filled with small change or candy. They are called Easter hags (*påskkärringar*), or Easter witches (*påskhäxor*) and they remind us that, according to Swedish folk beliefs, it was at Easter that the witches flew to a place called *Blåkulla* in order to meet with the devil and his lot in a blasphemous and lewd way – something which could result in the people who were singled out as witches being subjected to torture and hard punishment as late as in the mid-18th century.

However Swedes also unconsciously keep alive other remnants of beliefs in witches from times gone by. Particularly in western Sweden gunshots and firecrackers sound out in the dark Easter night, which is also illuminated by huge outdoor bonfires here and there. Both the shots and the bonfires are old, tried and true methods of keeping witches at bay.

Lent Switches and Easter Branches

Sometime before the turn of the last century there was a rumor circulating in a tiny community outside of Umeå that the new manager of the tar factory was a sadistic house tyrant who tormented children. Supposedly he had been seen by the villagers when he was cutting and breaking off birch branches. What else could birch branches be used for other than for whipping children?

What can we learn from this little story? Well, that the very popular Easter birch branches (*påskris*) were unknown – at least in the vicinity of Umeå – a century ago. We can actually determine rather accurately that Easter birch branches in their present form are a rather new holiday custom. However it is also one of the traditions that really thrives today – because they are as common now as Christmas trees or May poles. These are really several different older customs that have melded together into something modern. One of them was

The modern Easter branches (påskris) – preferably birch branches – are decorated with colorful feathers.

bringing birch branches inside into the warmth of the home during Lent so that the tiny leaves could be forced to sprout in time for Easter in order to create a sense of spring with some foliage.

Then there are the bare Lent switches, with no decorations or young leaves, which are meant to be used for whippings. This was an old custom on the morning of Good Friday – despite the extreme sanctity of the day – of carrying on early morning burlesque entertainment. The person who got up first had the right to use their switches to whip everyone else who still lazily lay in bed. This was meant to remind everyone of the suffering of Christ on this day. Usually it was the father of the household who carried out this symbolic form of corporal punishment, although sometimes it was the children who had the pleasure of whipping their parents. The farmhands preferred to whip the maids and vice versa. Whippings, something like a form of flirting between young people, also occurred at other times of the year.

The original Stockholm tradition that has now spread throughout Sweden – Easter birch branches decorated with feathers in many colors – most probably came about in the Stockholm area because the ordinary, undecorated birch branches that were brought indoors took on the colorful feather decorations of the Lent switches.

Easter Eggs

An Easter without Easter eggs, either real ones or artificial ones in more or less edible materials, is something that not only Swedes find difficult to imagine. No, there is no other food with "ritual" or religious connotations that is eaten in such great quantities by all Christians around the world during one or two days.

Of course you often hear popular speakers and priests explaining that Easter eggs are a symbol of the Resurrection of Christ, which is the culmination of the Easter miracle. Yes, we can accept this literal interpretation, however our egg orgies

during Easter have a completely different origin, even though it is connected to the church. In Sweden fasting at Lent is simply a word on the calendar. There is hardly anyone here who would forgo eating meat and eggs during the six weeks prior to Easter. Perhaps Swedes would allow Good Friday's dinner to be governed by tradition and let it consist of fish in the form of salmon, but a good Christian ought to abstain from the sauce or mayonnaise that is served along with it.

In the old days chickens were not the hatching machines that produce eggs all year round which they are today. The old farm hens had hormone peaks during several spring and summer months. It was this industrious egg laying that caused humans to utilize chickens. When the season for chicken eggs – and the wild bird eggs that people used to pilfer, mainly seagull and duck eggs – arrived it was also exactly when Lent

During Easter week Swedes eat 2,000 tons of eggs, and on Holy Saturday, the day before Easter, there are some 6,000 eggs on Swedish tables. This is when they usually paint their eggs in bright colors.

occurred, which meant that eggs could not be eaten then. They were stored in root cellars, and when Lent finally ended on Easter, quite obviously the menu was eggs and more eggs which Swedish country folk gladly washed down with swigs of vodka.

A Serving of Egg Statistics

During Easter week Swedes eat 2,000 tons of eggs, more than double the number eaten during a normal week. On Holy Saturday six million eggs are served on Swedish tables. But are you aware that while preparing for and celebrating Christmas even more eggs are consumed, cracked and mixed into all sorts of doughs and cake batters?

Every year the average Swede eats 200 eggs, of which 157 are boiled, poached or fried ("shelled eggs"), while the rest are used in preparing food. The average in the E. U. is even higher, 211 eggs per person annually.

Did you know that white chickens lay white eggs, and that colored hens lay brown ones, or that young chickens lay small eggs and old hens lay big ones?

Easter Lamb

One of the dishes that has become more common on the Easter menu is a garlic laced leg of lamb with Anglo-Saxon mint jelly. Paschal lamb is mentioned in the Book of Exodus, and previously people were happy to let it remain in that Old Testament setting. Now it just so happens that Sweden's native sheep have not been properly programmed to produce their offspring in time to serve as the raw material for Easter dinners.

No, the late introduction of Easter lamb on the Swedish holiday menu must instead be seen as a result of advances in freezing techniques and the modern transportation of fresh produce having eliminated the natural limitations of a great many of the seasonal eating habits and foods in days gone by. Sheep farmers from New Zeeland among others are those who Swedes can thank for the fact that this biblical expression can be concretized in today's practical culinary arts.

Once upon a time however roast mutton or lamb had traditional seasonal days even on Swedish tables, though this was at a point in time which was more suited to the yearly cycle of Nordic sheep. It was particularly around St. Bartholomew's Day, August 24, that lambs lived most dangerously every year.

The Easter Bunny

The Easter Bunny (*påskharen*) belongs to the rather recent elements in the profane Swedish celebration of Easter, one of the numerous holiday traditions imported from Germany. This is a kind of Easter Santa Claus who brings real or candy eggs. In its country of origin it was noted as early as the 17th century, but the first notation of an Easter bunny in Sweden is from 1901. In the beginning it was only among German immigrant families that eggs were hidden in apartments or in gardens so that the children in the household could try to find them. And when the German chocolate manufacturers and the Swedish pastry chefs discovered a slumbering Easter bunny market in Sweden we also got hollow chocolate bunnies in gaudy foil suits along with completely or partially chocolate coated marzipan rabbits to munch on.

But why a rabbit? The usual explanation is that Easter bread decorated with the Christian symbol of the Paschal lamb from southern Germany was misinterpreted when the shapes had become so distorted after baking that they were mistaken for rabbits.

Walpurgis Eve

Valborgsmässoafton

April 30

Long before students, temperance leagues, YMCA clubs, community centers and school teachers began to help a reluctant spring to get started in the way that we now consider to be very traditional, people's longing for sun and warmth was expressed in other ways. The celebration of Walpurgis Eve, or *Valborgsmässoafton*, was particularly widespread in southern Sweden where it is almost summer at that time of year. During the night of Walpurgis Eve young people in the villages in the provinces of Skåne and Blekinge would gather together in order to "bring the month of May to the village." Led by fiddlers they went from farm to farm and sang for a while outside the cottage windows.

Some of the group carried large baskets into which the farmers' wives could put the eggs, sausages, loaves of bread and bottles of vodka which the singers expected to receive as payment. On the next day, May 1, they would meet for their own party to eat, drink, dance and have fun.

When the time came to take up a collection to be able to pay the musicians, one of the farmhands went around with a plate and a bottle of vodka. Each person put a coin on the plate and got to take a swig from the bottle. The fiddler would play a May song as a receipt.

These begging traditions were also linked to other early summer festivities, although Walpurgis Eve was certainly the most dominant point in time.

The Swedish tradition of Valborg developed from the northern German witch bonfires. Since there were many Germans living in Stockholm during medieval times, it was there that the custom first took root. Today the Valborg bonfire is a genuine Swedish tradition.

Witches' Fires, May Bonfires and Walpurgis Bonfires

The only remains of Walpurgis celebrations that are left today are essentially the bonfires, with or without the accompanying songs. The latter feature is a late bourgeois addition to the tradition of gathering around a bonfire on the evening of April 30, and it most probably developed because of the way in which the students in Uppsala and Lund had celebrated the arrival of spring for more than 200 years. There are surely some people among the warmly dressed audiences who experience something that is almost magically infused with spring when songs such as "*Sköna maj, välkommen*" and "*Vintern rasat*" ring out in the darkness.

The bonfires actually have older origins. This was a very old custom in Sweden and in many other countries, lighting bonfires outdoors on some evening during the spring. It is not sure whether this was done to scare off predators in preparation for the grazing season for sheep and cows, or whether it was done for some supernatural, magical purpose such as when the Germans wanted to protect themselves from the witches who had gathered that night to worship the devil at Blocksberg. The Swedish custom has its origins in the northern German Walpurgis witch fires, and since the largest number of Germans could be found in and around Stockholm, it was also where it first took root. Our own witches were not completely idle on Walpurgis Eve, and it was said that they could be seen on this night sitting out in a stream holding empty butter churns between their knees. They frantically pounded their paddles while screeching at the top of their voices: "Good cow's milk in my pot!" In this way they could appropriate their neighbor's milk over the next year. If you happen to see this take place, you should load your rifle with salt, aim squarely at the witch's derriere and shoot while shouting: "Shit in your churn! Shit in your churn!" This thwarts her evil designs with the said results. It is definitely risky to be a witch!

Are our bonfires on Walpurgis Eve simply something we borrowed from the German fires to scare the witches away? Yes, some people have chosen to interpret them in this way, although this beautiful custom probably has an even older, local history. There are some folklorists who maintain that it ultimately has Celtic, or specifically Irish origins. May 1 was the first day of the summer half of the year in the ancient Celtic world in western Europe, and this was primarily celebrated with bonfires.

If you asked old folks why they built fires outside at this time of year, they would have most often answered that it was to scare away the wolves and the bears in the neighborhood so that they could put their animals out to pasture during the summer. There was an impressive symphony of noise that the industrious cattle farmers would produce on this day by using every means available to them. This was done so that they would dare to let their cows out the next day, since May 1 is the day for putting cows out to pasture throughout most of Sweden. So it was best if all of the wolves and bears had retreated back into the forest or up into the mountains. After that it would just be a matter of dealing with the foxes. However if the sheep were to be protected from them as well, then the master of the household would go out into the barn on Walpurgis Eve and urinate on them, after which they were made to step through a horse harness.

Walpurgis Predicts the Weather

The peculiar thing with this saint, whose eve we celebrate on the last day of April, is that she was not on the Swedish calendar until after 1901. Walpurgis existed earlier only as a kind of oral calendar tradition, something which is extremely unique. Walpurga, or Valborg in Swedish, was of the best repute, the daughter of an English king, who settled down as the abbess of Heidenheim Monastery in Germany. Apparently she did not make much of a mark during her lifetime, however after her death she behaved all the more like a saint. An oil dripped

Students in Uppsala and Lund and other cities have celebrated the arrival of spring for more than 200 years.

from her sarcophagus, and people who applied it were cured of all kinds of illnesses. This remarkable flow apparently continues to this day. Rationalist skeptics maintain that it is only the humidity which condenses on the cold gravestone, but before any of these pompous know-it-alls had appeared on the scene, the church had already canonized the good abbess. This took place on the first of May, and this subsequently became her feast day, which is especially observed in Germany. This is the reason why she became connected to the frenzy of spring celebrations in cities and throughout the countryside here in Sweden.

There are actually other indications of Walpurga or Valborg even after she was placed on the Swedish list of saints' legends, even though evangelical priests tried their best to banish such wild ideas. An old man in Älghult in the province of Småland told me about "Sanna Valbårra", as he called her. Oil flowed from her breast which could cure the sick. Perhaps this was a combination of the grave legend related above, and another continental tradition which maintained that Walpurga had a hole under her left breast which she got when Christ once exchanged hearts with her. Different versions of this operation are depicted in devout passion paintings in the Austrian pilgrimage churches.

"Are Walpurga's feet freezing?" If the answer to this question was yes, according to this saying, it meant that it would stay cold during the following forty nights in the province of Medelpad and elsewhere. She is freezing when there is frost outside on her night. In the old days at this time of year, farmers were extremely focused upon what the weather would be like during haymaking and harvest – much the way it is today, to some extent.

Following pages: Wood anemones (vitsippor) are in bloom, spring is here now!

The First of May

Första maj

The double celebration, the last of April and the first of May, was unique on the Swedish calendar (at least until our National Day was finally instituted as a civil holiday), a completely profane holiday with no religious links. It had its origins in ancient Rome, where an inspection of the armed forces was held on the Field of Martius, called the Campus Martius, on the first day of March, the month named after Mars, the Roman god of war. When the French kings adopted the same custom in the 8th century, it was impossible to conduct maneuvers in France because in March the roads there were in such disrepair and there was very little pastureland available for the cavalry horses. So the date had to be moved to the first of May, and it was called the May Field. This was when marksmanship and other knightly virtues were practiced.

As time went on these military maneuvers became outdated, although by then they had become a part of the festival customs in many northern European cities. The traditions continued on afterwards in more entertaining ways in the city guilds and spread farther away to other places including northern Europe. Like the city dwellers, the farmers held their village meetings on the same day, which thus became a holiday for their employees as well.

In 1940, the May 1st demonstration turned into a powerful manifestation of Swedish political unity in the shadow of World War II. This was the first time that red banners were intermixed with the blue and yellow Swedish flags.

The First of May became a work free weekday already during the Middle Ages, often the only one of the year (except for the free week at Michaelmas, the feast of St. Michael), and for this reason it naturally was designated as the workers' own day for outings in the country during the 1800s, and later on for political manifestations.

Since May 1 was a completely profane holiday it was given a rather unique position in the annual cycle of celebrations – all other holidays were simply holidays, religious feast days which each had their own particular cult. However the character of the first of May as a universal, happy holiday was preserved in our country into the 19th century. By then the older special customs had long been abandoned, although people celebrated the coming of spring in other festive ways. The university students in Lund and Uppsala had May parties, the origin of the present-day student carnivals. In Stockholm the entire bourgeoisie went to Djurgården, the largest park in the city, in order to stand in the crowds along the street and bow to King Karl XV, and later towards the end of the century, to his younger brother Oscar II, as the royal family came by in an open carriage or on horseback.

Labor Day

Of course there was a very different reaction when the working classes used the same holiday in order to congregate in huge groups waving red flags and union banners. Their meeting place, the antithesis of the Djurgården event, was Ladugårdsgärdet, another park in Stockholm. The idea of turning May 1 into a demonstration day for workers and socialists actually came from the United States. There the American Federation of Labor demanded eight hour work days in a spectacular way already from May 1, 1884, and when the Second International held their first congress in 1889, a delegation from the AFL launched a proposal that May 1 should be designated as the demonstration day for the international workers' movements.

The time came to realize this in Sweden already in 1890. The demonstrations attracted 20,000 participants in Stockholm and Malmö and 25,000 in Gothenburg. In addition there were numerous demonstration parades that were arranged in many provincial cities and manufacturing towns. The record was set in 1939 when May 1 was made a civil holiday and the demonstration parade gathered more than 170,000 participants in Stockholm. By then the shadow of Nazi Germany lay heavily over northern Europe, and the Swedish flag was carried at the head of the parade as a manifestation of national unity in the face of this threat.

During the "cold war" the crowds diminished, and demonstrations were cancelled in many places. However with a socialist government in place it did not seem necessary to go to the extreme of overthrowing the government. The transformation of the working class into the middle class also contributed to this diminishing interest. Besides, this holiday where everyone was off from work came at a perfect time for those who had

The May 1st demonstration parade of the Left Party in a small Swedish town.

community gardens, or those who were balcony gardeners, homeowners with gardens and summer cottage owners so they could take care of their respective plots. Thank goodness that we in our idyllic situation were not commandeered into the more militaristic, compulsory May 1 demonstrations like in the Communist Block. Although it makes one wonder, what was this day like before it became the workers' own day?

The May King

In a small announcement in the Stockholm City records from 1486 there can be found one of our earliest confirmations of Stockholmers celebrating May 1 by selecting a May King already in the Middle Ages – a spectacle that soon gained more respectable status and grew much larger in scale since the actual selection of the May King was carefully monitored and recorded by the city magistrate. It was something like the selection of Lucia, even though it was a man who was chosen, and just as the semi-official crowning of Lucia by today's newspapers has its counterpart in companies and associations, the journeymen in the larger trade guilds used to select their own May King and arrange their own First of May party somewhere in the vicinity of the town.

Shoot a Parrot on the First of May

Parrot competitions were also an old custom, and there is a notation in the Stockholm court records dated April 29, 1498 stating how these events were to be conducted. It was the duty of one of the city's guild societies, Our Lady's Guild or St. Gertrude's Guild, to see that a pole was erected which had a picture of a parrot attached on top.

The idea was to hit a bird fastened to the top of a high pole. The person who hit the target received as his reward the honor of wearing a silver parrot on a chain around his neck (there is an example of such a silver bird in the Historical Museum in Visby on the island of Gotland), and of treating all of the other participants to beer, which could turn out to be an expensive proposition. This marksmanship competition with crossbows or bows and arrows was by law only allowed on this particular day and on Pentecost Monday.

It was stipulated that the winner's expenses were not to exceed one last of beer. A last was equal to twelve barrels and each barrel contained 125 liters of beer, so it is perhaps understandable that the rules for awarding the prize in the parrot shooting contest made it a markedly upper class diversion, and also that this upper class was endowed with a very healthy thirst.

In some ways we still have a reminder of the parrot shooting competition on May 1 in a completely different and much more lively modern festive custom, namely the maypole.

The creator of the May flower (Majblomman) was Beda Hallberg (1869–1945) who was involved in aid work for children who had contracted tuberculosis. In 1907 she initiated a fundraising campaign by selling the first May flowers. They were a huge financial success. Later she became one of the leading forces in the fight against tuberculosis.

Following pages: These are the different color combinations which May flowers have had over the years. Today they are still sold before the first of May.

Warm Weather Before the First of May Brings Chilly Weather After

These were the ingredients for May 1 celebrations in our cities. What happened out in the countryside? In the lives of the landowning farmers and village communities the day played a role as an administrative new year's day, just as it did in the cities. Elders were chosen, accounting meetings were held and the peasants went around together and checked their fences. If someone had not done their part they were fined, usually in the form of beer which their comrades drank up.

Naturally there were also some folk beliefs and weather prophesies linked to such a special day on the calendar. As a prediction of the coming weather it was said that frogs would remain silent after the feast day of Walpurgis on May 1 for just as long as they had been heard to croak or rumble before that date, which could be interpreted like this: warm weather before the first of May would often be followed by a period of cold weather.

1907 1908 1909 1910 1911 1912 1913
1921 1922 1923 1924 1925 1926 1927
1935 1936 1937 1938 1939 1940 1941
1949 1950 1951 1952 1953 1954 1955
1963 1964 1965 1966 1967 1968 1969
1977 1978 1979 1980 1981 1982 1983
1991 1992 1993 1994 1995 1996 1997
2005 2006 2007 2008 2009 2010 2011

The First of May

Ascension Thursday

Kristi himmelsfärdsdag

39 Days After Easter

According to the Bible, this was the day that Christ left this earth and ascended into heaven. In the Swedish folk holiday traditions the purely religious elements are few and far between. Certainly there have been a number of such customs, however they were mostly linked to very profane purposes.

That is what has probably contributed to this holiday in the middle of a work week becoming a thorn in the side of businesses and government authorities who have managed to rid our calendar of most of these kinds of holiday anomalies. There has been talk of moving "Flying Day," as it is sometimes called, to the following Saturday or even better to Sunday. Such assaults on our traditions have thus far been rejected. The following Friday is probably the year's most utilized *klämdag* (a day following a mid-week holiday, see introduction) which creates a wonderful four day spring break for all kinds of outdoor activities, from walks to working on boats or raking leaves in the yard.

Temperance Day, which is organized by the Swedish Temperance League, has been celebrated on Ascension Day ever since 1925. This usually happens in the form of outdoor activities which are organized in some hundred places around the country.

Previously it was a bit touch and go with temperance on

this particular day. Back then this "Holy Thursday" was one of the most important religious days of the year for church-goers, though it had a particular character in that respect. In some provinces people would start to make something like courtesy calls to churches in other parishes. Often a bountiful market tradition would develop in connection with these outings, and jovial social interaction followed after the high mass. Picnic baskets and vodka were unpacked, emotions ran high, and soon it would be time for the first good fight of the season. This kind of church service is still practiced in some places, though in a much more subdued way.

A Day for Fishing Luck and Green Pastures

In almost all of Sweden there used to be an old rule that you could not begin fishing in the rivers and lakes before Ascension Thursday, and therefore it has also gone by the name "The First Angler Day."

Why was Ascension Thursday the day on which the annual fishing season began? One researcher has presented the idea that this was the day on which fishing gear was blessed in the medieval church before the beginning of the fishing season.

Cows had every reason to look forward to this "Holy Thursday" with delight because this was the day in many areas when cows were put out to pasture and the heifers who had not yet been named were christened.

In the provinces of Västergötland and Dalsland among other places, and in some parts of Värmland, it was customary earlier to have an Ascension Thursday bonfire outdoors. There was music and dancing around the fires until the early morning. Today this happens mainly in the area of Österlen in the southeastern part of the province of Skåne where Ascension Thursday bonfires still burn. There are different hypotheses about their original function. I myself tend to agree with a researcher who thought that people had bonfires for practical reasons, namely that bonfires were used to protect the newly sprouting crops in the fields from being damaged by frost.

Pentecost

Pingst

50 Days After Easter

The religious role of Pentecost as a kind of finale for the Easter celebration, with the descent of the Holy Ghost upon the apostles, has hardly managed to foster very much ecstatic religious emotion among ordinary people. Thus Pentecost has a less spectacular role in terms of popular spirituality in comparison to Christmas and Easter. With all due respect, the Holy Spirit has not been able to spark people's imaginations in the same way as the romantic message of Christmas or the solemn lesson of Easter. Of course this does not mean that Pentecost lacks religious associations in other ways. More on this later.

Up until 2005 Pentecost provided a welcome relief in the form of a work free holiday over a good long spring weekend. However patriotically inclined government authorities reduced it to a perfectly normal weekend in order to make our National Day on June 6 a red letter day on the calendar. In preindustrial peasant society Pentecost Monday meant a work free day that came at a time of the year when the heavy labors of spring planting, such as fertilizing and plowing, were finished and the summer harvest had not yet begun. For young people, Pentecost was a time for leisure, dancing and flirting.

Getting married during the Pentecost weekend – an ecstatic time – is a very old Swedish tradition.

Youth Clubs and Pentecost Brides

Most notable during the celebration of Pentecost in earlier times were the clubs for young people because they had their own particular structure during this weekend.

In 1746 some stern local residents in Utby village in the province of Västergötland complained about the village youth who had "carried on indecently during the actual church service with a so-called Pentecost bride dressed in disguise, etc." There are many reports from earlier times from all around Sweden, particularly in the south, of young people dressing up as Pentecost brides and grooms in order to celebrate a Pentecost wedding.

This involved riding the bridal couple through the village and showing off their splendid finery at each farm, in hopes of collecting all sorts of favors both in liquid and in solid form. With two mounted attendants leading the way, the bridal procession went from farm to farm singing a song and collecting gifts. There were bridesmaids and groomsmen in pairs following the bridal couple, and behind them a row of girls in pairs holding straw baskets into which eggs, pork, bread, butter and bottles could be placed.

Older folklorists considered this bridal custom at Pentecost to be a remnant of pagan fertility rites, or perhaps something even worse than that. Yet their context is much less complex. The finest thing people could dress up as in the old days was in fact a bridal couple, and this was something that had to be done in order to entice one's neighbors to be generous. Certainly there is no reason to try to find a deeper meaning in the floral brides and garlanded grooms at Pentecost.

A Time of Ecstasy

Pentecost is the only major holiday in Sweden which has no national culinary tradition to showcase.

Even though the religious significance of Pentecost was not very interesting to ordinary people, Pentecost Day developed into a major day for churchgoing. This was the most important day for giving alms, although the aim of the church visit was mainly to give women a chance to show off their summer finery. Particularly for children, the walk to church through the verdant spring landscape with a little bouquet of daffodils or cowslips in their hands would become the memory of a lifetime. There was a prevalent old wives' tale that a woman who wanted to become pregnant during the following months of the year should bring a child with them to church on this particular day. If you did not have your own child, you could borrow one from a neighbor, it was thought that this would have the same effect.

The often quoted lines written by the author Esaias Tegnér (1782-1846) about Pentecost being "a time of ecstasy" referred of course to the emotions of the young confirmation candidates who were to receive their First Communion, however there was also widespread ecstasy of another kind than what the bishop had in mind. As a matter of fact in many areas it was considered acceptable for the newly confirmed young people to go to parties and dances with their peers, so that the evening of Pentecost Monday was often the time when newcomers would be introduced to the amusements of the young people's community.

Predicting Weather and Pentecost Rain

Most everyone, including all of the Pentecost brides, would probably agree that it was best if there was beautiful weather during Pentecost. This holds true even today – Pentecost is the perfect time to work on your summer cottage or boat or to care for your garden. In old times people did not think about such aspects in relation to the weather at Pentecost. There are two conflicting attitudes which can be found in the old documents. "Rain at Pentecost seldom does any good," was said in some places, a direct quotation from the *Farmer's Almanac*, the old handbook for farmers. In other places it seemed as though rain at Pentecost was just what the farmer wanted, and there

public opinion was unanimous: "Rain at Pentecost and sunshine at Midsummer are worth barrels of gold," as the saying went. By comparing both of these desires with our Nordic climate and the Nordic agrarian year it is clear that the expectations of rain at this time of year are very well founded. The fear of rain at Pentecost in the *Farmer's Almanac* made sense in southern Germany where it originated, because that time of year was often when the grain was blooming at its peak, which meant rain could destroy the crops. The fear of rain is an example of how the *Almanac* managed to enrich Nordic folklore with completely incorrect weather prognoses.

In fact it is strange that a moveable feast such as Pentecost should be used for such things as predicting weather – within Sweden there can be a variation in time of almost an entire month, and this happens at a point in the year when the difference in climate between southern and northern Scandinavia is quite extreme.

May, illustration by Elsa Beskow, one of Sweden's most beloved illustrators of children's books, 1927.

EB

Mother's Day

Mors dag

4th Sunday in May

In many respects Mother's Day is a controversial day to celebrate. Just as with Father's Day, some people consider it to be extremely inappropriate both psychologically and socially in light of all of the families where one of the parents is missing. Others criticize it because it is a modern, marketing device for the profit of florists, bakeries and candy makers, as well as an expression of American commercialism.

However things are not quite that simple. Mother's Day has very old origins in folk traditions, although perhaps not in Sweden. It has long been held sacred, particularly in England. Already in the beginning of the 17th century the fourth Sunday in Lent was called Laetare Sunday there, or Mothering Sunday (*midfastosöndagen* in Swedish): *a day to celebrate mothers*. It had in fact been given that name because people were supposed to "go a-mothering." This originally meant that you were supposed to visit the "mother church" of your parish, namely the church from which one's own church had once been established. However the religious historical interpretation of "mother" was soon forgotten, and there was a transition to a more tangible, familiar meaning.

Early on this particular "Mothering Day" also assumed a profane interpretation of the word "mother," and already in the 1600s there was a well established tradition in England that children were supposed to visit their parents on Mothering Sunday, particularly if they had to move away to find work.

A lilac bush in bloom.

Ann Jarvis (1854–1948) was a teacher and the daughter of an American Methodist minister. She established, or rather re-established, an old Anglo-Saxon Mother's Day tradition at the beginning of the 20th century.

Ann Jarvis Creates Mother's Day

Having some type of family celebration sometime in the spring, a kind of family reunion, has become very traditional in a number of European countries. Often it was the head of the family, usually the oldest female member, who gathered her offspring together for a festive meal.

Due to the influence of the term "Mothering Day," particularly in England, it came to be one's own mother that people wanted to honor.

However it was in Philadelphia that the modern Mother's Day was created by an American teacher, Ann Jarvis (1864-1948). In 1907 (or perhaps 1908, sources differ), she convinced her parish priest there to conduct a service with a sermon about the fourth commandment with a particular focus on loving one's Mother. She decorated the church with white carnations and handed them out afterwards to all of the parishioners who attended the service. Ann Jarvis continued to be an energetic advocate of her Mother's Day idea, for already in 1914 she enjoyed the triumph of having President Wilson establish the second Sunday in May, the date of her own mother's death, as an official holiday on the American calendar.

Of course that country's businessmen smelled the scent of money, money when this happened. Advertising campaigns for suitable Mother's Day presents became ever more insistent, and Mother's Day cards spread like a plague. There are not many days when American restaurants are so fully booked as on Mother's Day. It was said that Aunt Ann was actually quite distressed by the commercialization of the day which she had intended to be so harmonious. And when Mother's Day turned out to be such a successful commercial venture, then Father's Day was quickly established as well, and of course also Brother's, Sister's and even a dog's day, which thankfully did not last very long.

Based on the American model, Mother's Day was introduced in Europe – or rather it was re-introduced since Mothering Day and its counterparts on the continent most certainly were the prototype – during the first years after the World War I in most countries, as it also was in Sweden, on the fourth Sunday in May.

Here in Sweden it was the feminist writer Cecilia Bååth-Holmberg who launched Mother's Day. Due to the notoriety of the name of its female originator at that time, the idea of Mother's Day had a huge impact and was quickly adopted by newspapers and magazines.

Mother's Day Meets Resistance

No annual holiday has met with so much criticism and opposition from different popular movements as Mother's Day. The film star Shirley MacLaine was at the forefront of the Emergency Committee to Boycott Mother's Day in the U. S. during the 1970s, and at the same time in Copenhagen the "Red Stockings" organized anti-Mother's Day demonstrations because according to them it had to do with reactionary definitions of sexual roles. In Sweden child psychologists thundered about this commercial gimmick, and several Social Democratic women's groups wanted to ban the celebration.

To a certain extent the questioning of the celebration of Mother's Day was the result of the fate of this old new custom in Germany. In 1939 the state assumed control of the celebration of *Der Tag der deutschen Mutter*, where one of the highlights was Hitler's granting of a Cross of Honor, an *Ehrenkreutz,* to the mothers who brought outstanding numbers of little Arians into the world. In 1946 the German Mother's Day was understandably silenced, although it was revived in 1947 in West Germany in a form with no undertones or medals for family propagation.

DEN 6 JUNI
G. Ankarcrona
1916.
SVENSKA FLAGGANS DAG
STADION · SKANSEN

The National Day of Sweden

Sveriges nationaldag

For a very long time Swedes insisted that they were perhaps the only country in the world which did not have an official national day. That so many people would brag about this deficiency can certainly be seen as symptomatic of the skepticism Swedes have for patriotic manifestations in general. There had been attempts made as early as the 19th century to launch this kind of commemorative day among the echelons of society who fostered the idea of nationalism.

A Skansen Event

At the end of the 19th century the waves of national romanticism ran high and many enthusiasts felt that Sweden should also have an official National Day. One of the first steps in this direction was taken by Artur Hazelius, the founder of the open air museum Skansen and the Nordiska Museum in Stockholm, where the celebration of Swedish Flag Day (*Svenska flaggans dag*) began in 1892 with a ceremony that was held at Skansen. The date that he chose was June 6, with the motivation that this was the date when a parliament in the town of Strängnäs crowned Gustav Vasa as King of Sweden whereby Sweden withdrew from the Kalmar Union which had united the three

June 6

In 1892 Artur Hazelius – the creator of Skansen, the open-air museum in Stockholm – began to celebrate the Swedish Flag Day on June 6 at Skansen. In 1983 this date was finally made Sweden's National Day. However it was not until 2005 that June 6 became a red letter day on the Swedish calendar, making it a work free holiday.

A poster by the artist Gustaf Anckarcrona, 1916.

countries of Sweden, Denmark and Norway. However June 6 was also the date when the Instrument of Government of 1809 was signed, which ended the absolute reign of the heirs of Gustav Vasa, and in many ways this meant the beginning of the democratization of Sweden's government. For a long time the day remained the "Swedish Flag Day" which merely was an event at Skansen with a limited range of interest.

A National Day – At Last

June 6 was finally given the status of the official National Day in 1983. Note well that when it was established, this modest display of nationalism was marked by the fact that the National Day was an ordinary work day. The flag ceremonies with speeches which were arranged in many places were therefore held in the evening – as was the King's distribution of flags at Skansen – although this was nothing like the popular festivities such as those held in Norway on May 17. On the other hand however, there are very few countries equipped with so many private flag poles as in Sweden, which is why there are yellow and blue flags waving in most yards and gardens, at summer cottages and on apartment balconies and sail boats on the other days such as Midsummer Day and the like which are marked on the Swedish calendar as flag days.

A pastry for Sweden's National Day.

King Carl XVI Gustaf on June 6, together with Queen Silvia, Crown Princess Victoria and Princess Madeleine, who are all dressed in the Swedish National costume.

The definitive proclamation of the National Day as a public holiday (as compared to its forerunner May 1!) took place in 2005, and it is now noted as a red letter day on the Swedish calendar.

Very soon a new typically Swedish topic of discussion arose: whether the new National Day ought to be celebrated with a special national dish, something with a grander culinary flourish than the sugary sweet Gustav Adolf's pastry served in foggy November. Does Sweden not have a appropriate national dish such as Hungarian goulash or Spanish paella? The answer to this question will probably be just as long in coming as it took for our National Day to make it through the door.

Zero Sette

Midsummer

Midsommar

Friday
June 19–June 25

Of all the European countries today it is currently only Sweden and Finland which celebrate Midsummer so exhaustingly that it motivates an extra day as a holiday in order to be able to recuperate from being up all night. Nevertheless June 24 is a day of celebration throughout most of the Christian world, and has been so for at least 1,500 years – though with no May poles, except in Swedish areas. Therefore we should first take a look at the actual holiday itself, to then discover the roots of our special tradition: the Midsummer pole decorated with foliage, which has a completely different origin.

The Feast Day of St. John the Baptist

June 24, the "correct Midsummer Day," the one which we Swedes celebrated up until 1951, is the feast day of St. John the Baptist on the calendar, the same name it has in all Christian countries. Nowadays "Midsummer Day" is noted on the Swedish calendar as a red letter day on the Saturday that falls closest to June 24.

In almost all of Europe – and in some places quite far away from our part of the world – St. John the Baptist's feast day is celebrated in exactly the same way, namely with a bonfire outdoors. The first known St. John's bonfire was lit at the beginning of the 6th century in Tunis. Swedes were no different,

Folk musicians in the province of Dalarna during Midsummer celebrations.

we followed the same traditions. But why light bonfires at Midsummer?

In all probability the church helped to spread this custom already in the early Middle Ages, and perhaps an even older, pre-Christian tradition at this time of year might have been the source. Instead of forbidding heathen celebratory customs, the medieval church often adopted them and let them live on after they had been given more respectable Christian contents, for example by linking it to the worship of some saint. In some places reference was made to the words which the evangelist Matthew put into the mouth of St. John: "He who follows me … shall baptize you with the Holy Spirit and fire."

Left: Raising a large Maypole – which is supposed to be as tall as possible – is heavy work. This one is in the village of Övre Gärdsjö outside the town of Rättvik.

Whatever the case might be – there were probably Midsummer bonfires already in pre-Christian times, and in all likelihood their explanation comes from the position of Midsummer day in the astronomical year: on the June 21 or 22. The summer solstice occurs a few days earlier when the sun rises to the highest point in the heavens whereupon the days once again begin to get shorter. In cultures with sun worship (of which there are many) it is important to observe the different positions of the sun during the year, and it would be plausible for a primitive magical way of thinking to "nurture" the sun during the summer solstice by lighting warming fires outdoors.

A man from Dalarna (dalmas) dressed in the traditional Rättvik costume, and a woman from Dalarna (dalkulla) dressed in a folk costume from the village of Boda.

The May Pole – A German Story

Our Midsummer pole also has a long history. The chapter on the first of May tells about the Franks' "May Field" (the Franks were Germanic peoples). Among the shooting competitions which were practiced at that time was one which involved shooting a bow and arrow at a high pole with a target attached, a picture of a bird that was called a parrot. Only God knows why (etymologists do not know the answer in any case). These practices spread throughout western Europe during the Middle Ages.

When this custom of parrot shooting arrived in the Germanic countries during the 13th century it met with another custom that had a long history, namely that on a weekday in May people would decorate (to *maja* in Swedish) their homes with greenery: young birch leaves, branches with leaves and flowers. The Swedish verb *maja* comes from the Latin name of the month of May, *Maius, or maj* in Swedish, the month that was dedicated to the Roman god Jupiter Maius. So even the pole with the parrot was decorated with flowers and leaves – and there you have the May pole, or *majstång* in Swedish! There is often a rooster or some other bird on the top of the German May poles, a vestige of the earlier bird target.

During the Middle Ages large numbers of Germans moved to Sweden in order to take advantage of the natural resources and the trade opportunities which Swedes were unable to exploit themselves. They settled mainly in the eastern Swedish cities, in the mining district of Bergslagen as well as around Lake Mälaren, where they came to dominate both politics and culture in many ways. Of course they also brought their German holiday and festival customs and practices with them, which Swedes began to imitate. A long list of our most popular traditions originated from these Germans. As for the first of May tradition, there was much that could easily be adopted even in Sweden, however when it came time to decorate the May pole it proved difficult to find enough flowers and greenery at that time of year. In this situation the popular custom with the May pole was not abandoned, instead it was moved to a time of the year when there was plenty of decorative material in nature, Midsummer. This is why our Midsummer pole is often called by its German name, a May pole.

Midsummer Dance (Midsommardans), painted by Anders Zorn, 1897.

Following pages: Midsummer in Sweden, 2010.

The term Midsummer pole was first mentioned in 1635, and in the 1660s and 1670s when Erik Dahlbergh made drawings for his illustrated work, *Ancient and Modern Sweden* (*Suecia Antiqua et Hodierna, Det forna och nutida Sverige*), you can often see these typical poles rising up above the horizon of

the roofs in the cityscapes depicting eastern Sweden. This was not because his drawings were all made right around Midsummer, rather it was because the poles back then were left to stand year round – as later became the case in many places such as Dalarna.

From the towns and the manor houses in central Sweden (*Mellansverige* as it is called), this festival custom spread throughout the countryside where it was quickly accepted since it was both spectacular and easily organized. Often it was the young people in the village who took care of the arrangements. Villages competed with one another to see who had the tallest and finest May pole.

The clergy did not approve of this way of celebrating a Christian holiday, and the religious "revival" movement of the 19th century was just as negative. Many of the permanent Midsummer poles were chopped down by these "orthodox" believers. Fortunately the pleasure seekers triumphed over the dreary religious ranks, and so it was that one of the Swedish celebration traditions which had acquired an international reputation was allowed to survive.

Today the Midsummer pole – completely incorrectly as a matter of fact – is considered to be a genuine Swedish tradition with its roots in Dalarna.

Strawberries are the traditional dessert on Midsummer's Eve.

The Oracle of Love and White Nights

Those who stay at home in their houses and row house communities often get together on Midsummer's Eve so that that they and their children can decorate the Midsummer pole on a lawn, and then spend the afternoon playing games and frolicking with the children. Later in the evening it is time for the adult entertainment in the backyards, on the verandas or under the porch roofs of the campers. During this white night it is not difficult to understand that the idea of Midsummer bonfires would have been rather pointless at our latitudes.

No other night has been so closely associated with the

oracle of love as this one. Everyone knows about the trick of placing flowers under your pillow in order to dream about your future spouse, however you cannot just do this randomly if you want to be assured of results.

Back when girls (because it was actually only young ladies who were curious) took this very seriously, tradition demanded that you should follow certain rules which varied from place to place. In some places it was said that seven or nine flowers had to be picked from the fields on the same number of farms, or that they all should have names that began with the same letter (a clue: v is a good choice!), or that they should be gathered between sundown and midnight (more difficult the farther north you go!). If this was done correctly you would dream about your intended fiancé, although you could also discover something about how a future marriage would turn out. To this aim you had to place three glasses on your bedside table before going to bed, one with water, one with wine and one with vodka. Then your dream prince was supposed to empty one of the glasses before your dream ended, as it was believed. If it was the glass of water you could expect a good, but rather boring life. If he chose the glass of wine the marriage would be more fun, but if he downed the snaps you risked getting a husband who was a drunk.

But those who suffer from hay fever can never even get to sleep because of their constant sneezing and sniveling. Luckily there were other ways for them. A popular alternative was to eat dream herring. Right before going to bed you were supposed to eat a whole salted herring, head, fins, innards, tail and all, that had not been soaked to remove the salt. Early the next morning you would awaken extremely thirsty and would then see your intended husband come and offer you something to quench your thirst, after which you would have the same possibility of guessing your fate according to what he poured into the glass.

For those who are sensitive there is yet another method: to eat dream pancakes. Here three girls together were supposed to make a dough of salt, water and flour and then each girl had to fry and eat a thin pancake. But this method was complicated by the fact that they were not allowed to talk, laugh or sing, because then it would not work. This requirement was probably extremely difficult for giddy teenage girls to fulfill.

Midsummer night also had its risks, especially for young and innocent girls who could be lured by its mystique. The Midsummer dance was mainly a party for young people where love played an important role. It used to be in some places that a girl could not say no when asked to follow her fiancé to the sleeping loft on Midsummer night. So there certainly must have been some foundation for the proverbial saying: "Midsummer night is not very long, but it sets many cradles to rocking along."

Sill and New Potatoes – Newcomers to Our Traditions

Every holiday has its own traditional food, some of which is quite old-fashioned. However the modern menu for Midsummer celebrations, pickled herring and new potatoes followed by strawberries and ice cream, is not very old. In earlier times people would make a feast out of a bowl of cultured milk (*filbunke*) or *lutfisk*. There was certainly no shortage of herring, quite the opposite, but at a time when people were forced to eat salt herring every day of the year it was difficult to stomach herring being elevated to a festive dish. Cultured milk or *filbunke* was at least something you had to forego all through winter because there was no milk to be had when the cows had stopped giving milk. So it seemed quite festive to be able to become reacquainted with cultured milk. *Lutfisk* was party food not only at Christmas, but also at weddings and funerals, no matter what the season. Only "fine" food gave status to a party because it was bought at a store in town – the kind of "store-bought food" that people could not afford every day.

Sill (pickled herring) and new potatoes with "snaps".

Before it was absolutely out of the question for normal people to eat fresh potatoes so early, for this was considered to be wasting God's gifts at a time when crops could fail in

Sweden. So no one dug up potatoes until they got as big as possible. Eating them when they were the size of plums would have been considered a terrible sin. No, our Midsummer orgies today are certainly a product of our times, because we would never think along those lines today.

Crayfish Parties

Kräftskivor

The Discovery of the Delicious Crayfish

August

One of the first Swedish notations of crayfish is a recipe from 1522 where Bishop Peder Månsson, Sweden's first true scientist, recommended crayfish dissolved in vodka for treating cholera. The world-famous natural scientist Carl von Linné cautioned against eating shellfish at all. From the considerable number of times they are mentioned in his writings it is clear that he was allergic to shellfish and that he got hives whenever he tried to eat them. So of course it is quite understandable that he would label these gifts of nature as unfit for human consumption.

Luckily he had little success with these efforts – 18th century Swedes belonging to the category known as "the gentility" loved shellfish and definitely were not prepared to refrain from eating them. The 18th century enthusiasm for crayfish was not a fad, instead its origins were the changes in eating habits which came in the wake of the Renaissance and which subsequently were refined by French cuisine. Because of this, fishing for crayfish gradually became an important source of income in many parts of Sweden, although one should not believe that country folks could eat what they caught. No, crayfish were food for the upper class, as were mushrooms, and that was that.

A platter piled high with crayfish with the obligatory accompaniment, snaps.

Following pages: This classic idyllic Swedish painting, Fishing Crayfish (Kräftfiske), was painted by Carl Larsson in 1894. It depicts the late summer festival, the crayfish party (kräftskivan), which was and is still celebrated – in the archipelagos or even in the close company of one's own family by a private lake stocked with crayfish.

Now the aroma of the northern European "purebred crayfish" is quite superior to its continental cousins, and because of this it became an important export product as time went on.

Barrels of salt cured crayfish tails from Lake Hjälmaren were sent to German luxury restaurants among other places, and already in the 1870s the cookbook author Charles Emil Hagdahl shuddered at the probable destiny of Swedish crayfish: that they would be fished to depletion. He did not know just how right he was. It is really sad to consider how one of our major culinary assets has almost become extinct, even though the crayfish plague played a larger role in this than crayfish traps did. One hundred years ago Sweden was Europe's leading exporter of crayfish, now we are outstanding as the major importer, and this has resulted in crayfish successively becoming threatened in the new countries which we have turned to in order to satisfy our unique craving for crayfish.

A Swedish Tradition is Created

What you just read should not induce my readers to believe that Swedes have indulged in crayfish parties with vodka and funny hats in the glow of smiling paper moon lanterns – far from it. When people did eat crayfish *au naturel* in olden times, they were usually freshly cooked and warm.

These days there are many Swedes who have no idea what a delicacy they are missing. Sometime in the 18th or 19th century Swedes changed the temperature of the crayfish they served, and together with the late 19th century romanticism of summer cottages and archipelagos (among those who had the means), there also arose the typical Swedish crayfish party with all of its extra accoutrements and an abundance of vodka shots.

In the old days consuming crayfish was nothing that was primarily done in August, crayfish were available year round. However when crayfish fishing began to reach vast proportions (5 million crayfish were pulled up annually from Lake Hjälmaren!) it was necessary to protect these coveted treats

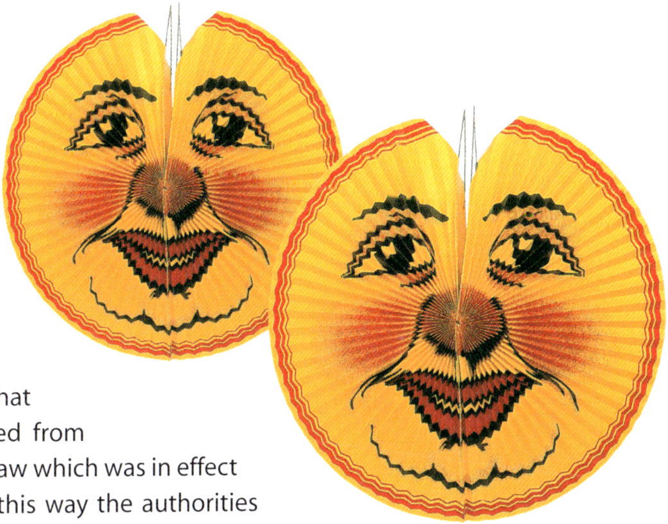

from extinction, particularly while they were molting and spawning. During the 1800s the first county-wide ordinances appeared which generally forbade crayfish fishing from April until the beginning of August. This gradually went into effect nationwide and it was established that crayfish fishing was prohibited from November 1 until August 8, a law which was in effect until just a few years ago. In this way the authorities created the foundation for something festive, the most Swedish thing of all including the May pole, namely the premier crayfish party in the beginning of August. Even though it is now possible to buy crayfish year round, at least frozen ones, there are not many people who want to think about them in any other way than as the culinary culmination of August. It certainly seems strange to have to praise something as awful as bureaucracy. However – we must give credit where credit is due, even in this case.

Following pages: Autumn is on its way.

Fermented Herring Day

Surströmmingsdagen

3rd Thursday in August

When Danes want to motivate their opinions about Swedes as being barbaric people, it is usually corroborated by referring to both fermented herring or *surströmming* and *lutfisk*, a Christmas delicacy made of dried salted fish, as evidence. Finns in the same situation are content with only noting the former delicacy since they, our neighbors to the east, actually enjoy eating *lutfisk* as well.

Open Carefully!

Surströmming – which you either love or you hate, *tertium non datur* – has, after a light salting, been subjected to the same curing process as the original cured salmon, *gravad lax*, and the popular Norwegian fermented fish called *rakefisk*, in particular fermented trout. When the fermentation process has started the herring is kept cool for six to seven weeks before it is ready to be consumed. These days almost all *surströmming* is sold in cans. It is produced mainly in Ulvöhamn on the island of Norra Ulvö, along *Högakusten*, the High Coast in the northern province of Ångermanland which borders on the Baltic Sea.

Fermented herring (surströmming) now has its own postage stamp.

The production processes of fermenting fish to make *surströmming* and *rakefisk* are local relics of a very old method of preserving food. It has completely disappeared in Finland, although Carl Linnaeus confirmed that it also existed there in the 18th century. Another clue is the very well-known Finnish fermented herring or *Sursill*. Of course Icelandic fermented shark also belongs to the same family.

In the past fermented herring could not be sold over the counter in Sweden until the third Thursday in August, and as was the case with crayfish, most of the enthusiasts of this ancient dish wait until the right day before they (carefully!) insert a can opener into their bulging tin can. There are still many people, mainly from the north of Sweden, *norrlänningar*, who fully appreciate this peculiar aroma.

Surströmming (fermented herring) is eaten with tunnbröd (Swedish unleavened bread), potatoes, sour cream and red onions.

These days almost all fermented fish (surströmming) is sold in cans and is produced on the island of Norra Ulvö which is located in the Baltic Sea along the High Coast (Höga kusten) in the northern province of Ångermanland.

Thin unleavened bread called tunnbröd is traditionally baked in a wood burning brick oven.

Michaelmas, the Feast of St. Michael

Mickelmäss

September 29

The period after summer has very few celebrations and holidays. This was certainly a result of it being a time full of long and arduous labor performed by the country folk who made up the large majority of the population in Sweden: haymaking and harvest, threshing and slaughtering, preparing flax and producing butter, cheese, bread and drinks. Of course this did not mean that summer and autumn lacked joyful and festive occasions, however they were not regulated by the calendar of the church year but rather by the work year. Farm employees had the right to a "work-free week" and they received their annual wages in connection with Michaelmas, the feast of St. Michael, and the harvest. It was no coincidence that the number of markets culminated during the months around Michaelmas – when there was plenty of money in circulation.

During the month of September the apples are harvested while the red lingonberries ripen in the forest.

The ancient tradition of work related celebrations has almost died out these days, something which the Swedish food industry has long tried to change. It was thought that a food-related holiday was needed around this time of year. So many years ago the feast of St. Michael, Michaelmas was launched as a harvest festival with a rich offering of foodstuffs.

All Saints' Day and All Souls' Day

Alla helgons dag

In the 8th century the Roman Catholic Church began to celebrate November 1 as the feast day for all of the saints and martyrs, and this has continued to this day.

Saturday
Oct 31–Nov 6

The Saints' Own Day

There are a great many saints of varying degrees of importance, however not all of them have been assigned feast days on the calendar. November 1 was the day when the all of the saints, both great and small, were celebrated. Even though the Swedish Lutheran Church was totally uninterested in worshiping saints after the Reformation in the 16th century, they kept All Saints' Day in the ecclesiastical year, and even left it as a holiday. This was the case until 1772 when the Swedish King Gustav III moved it to the closest following Sunday which thereby became All Saints' Day.

In 1953 both the Swedish National Church Council and the Parliament thought that we had too few holidays between

All Souls' Day was celebrated in Sweden already during the 12th century. People commemorate deceased family members and pray for their souls. Decorating the graves of relatives with grave lanterns and wreaths on All Saints' Day is a tradition which we inherited more recently from Catholic countries.

Midsummer and Christmas, not a single one as a matter of fact. So in order to create a better balance of holidays, the Church Council reinstituted All Saints' Day as a revival of the old autumn religious holiday which was to be celebrated on the Saturday closest to October 31. However they kept the name *All Saints' Day* on the calendar for November 1, and this the original All Saints' Day usually falls on an regular weekday.

As though things were not complicated enough, the Abbot Odilo from the famous monastery of Cluny in Burgundy, came upon the idea that the following day, November 2, should be devoted to commemorating all of the deceased family members and offering prayers for their souls and all other departed souls. We know that this was celebrated in Sweden already at the end of the 12th century. During the Reformation in the 16th century the Swedes eliminated All Souls' Day from the ecclesiastical year, however today's direct connection to the dead and thereby to ghosts has of course contributed to the emergence of a number of later traditions during this double holiday. In the Swedish Church the idea of a day for souls has thus been revived in a sense, because the deceased are the theme of the service on the Sunday following All Saints' Day according to a Church ruling from 1983.

Skeletons, Goblins and Ghosts

Yet we definitely must add a little more paganism to this picture in order to make it complete. Among the ancient Britons, the Celtic people who lived in England when our era began, October 31 was considered to be the last day of summer. The Britons believed that on that night evil spirits, particularly goblins, were present so they used to light fires outdoors to drive out such demons. This tradition was adopted by the Angles and the Saxons from Germany who invaded England in the 6th century and drove out the Celts. Over time English children's pranks gradually developed from this tradition. Today this involves making jack-o'-lanterns by removing the insides of pumpkins – rutabagas were used in the old days – and carving them to look like skulls. The children then celebrate Halloween, *Helgonaafton* in Swedish, the evening before All Saints' Day when they go around to the neighbors and shout, "Trick or treat!" Of course this is a kind of extortion which is meant to result in gifts of candy or money. They sing a little jingle in thanks for the goodies. Englishmen took this custom with them to the United States, and it is from there that we in Sweden have imported it to our country as a new popular tradition. The idea of carving out skulls and illuminating them with candles inside actually existed in the province of Skåne in southern Sweden at least a century earlier, though sugar beets were used for the heads and there were no attempts at extortion.

Candles for the Deceased

There is also a more serious and beautiful tradition on All Saints' Day, which is to decorate the graves of deceased relatives with evergreens and wreathes and candles, a custom that we adopted a generation ago from Catholic countries to the south of us. In the beginning, the strict Protestant Swedish priests were not very happy with this Catholic practice, however it quickly spread across the country, mainly with the help of mass media and hardware stores wishing to sell grave lanterns. Candles on graves were not completely new, this had previously been done at Christmas, and nowadays most people probably consider All Saints' Day to be the correct day for this. Recently some churches have even adopted a new variation of this candle tradition: during a commemorative service one candle is lit for each member of the parish who died during the past year. As a result many churches are well-filled.

Father's Day

Fars dag

2nd Sunday in November

Father's Day, like Mother's Day, was imported from the U. S. A., and it allegedly originated in the state of Washington. It was there in 1910 that a Mrs. Dodd was supposed to have staged a celebration in honor of her aged father who as a young man had become a widower left alone with seven children.

A Tie for Father

A tie is a typical Father's Day present.

If this information is correct, the celebration of Father's Day apparently is not much younger than the modern form of Mother's Day celebrations. This new "day" appeared in Sweden in 1931, about the same time as in the other Nordic countries. In 1949, in an orderly Scandinavian manner and on the initiative of the merchants' associations, an inter-Nordic committee was assigned to investigate the best date for a universal Nordic celebration of Father's Day. They suggested the second Sunday in November, though even this has proved unsuccessful, like most coordinated efforts of this kind. In Sweden we have kept the agreed upon date, which is when wives and children spread a little light in the autumn darkness by serving morning coffee in bed. In some families, even a bouquet of flowers on the grave of a deceased father belongs to this tradition.

The most popular Father's Day present in Sweden is a tie, and stores featuring men's clothing stock up accordingly.

However ties are expensive today, so when younger children congratulate their fathers it is usually in the form of a Father's Day card. For a while Father's Day was considered old-fashioned and almost an asocial phenomenon in a culture where many children live in families with only one parent, and the father is usually the one missing in everyday life. Even so, stationary stores report that more and more Father's Day cards are sold each year. In any case, Father's Day has never achieved the same popularity as Mother's Day.

"November is very long and dreary," illustration by Birger Lundquist, 1947.

Martin

Mårten

Martin Was A Bishop

November 11

Already during the Middle Ages the combination of geese and the St. Martin celebration was inspired by the legends about Bishop Martin of Tours – he died on November 9, 397 and was buried on November 11 which became his feast day. It was said that Martin was a Roman soldier who became a Christian hermit, and the local people wanted to appoint him as bishop. Martin himself was not particularly interested in the job, and he hid among the geese so that he could avoid the people and their demands. However the cackling of the geese revealed where he was and Martin was ordained as bishop. This is why geese are eaten on St. Martin's Day, as a kind of punishment for their disloyalty, or so the saying goes.

A goose is something of a symbol for the province of Skåne in southern Sweden, and roast goose is a kind of symbolic "provincial dish" in Skåne. The artist Bertil Lybeck illustrated Selma Lagerlöf's tale about Nils Holgersson, the boy from Skåne who rode on the back of the lead goose as the flock flew over Sweden.

There are many indications that the continental practice of eating goose on the eve of St. Martin's Day has very old origins, for the first Martin's goose surfaced on the historical duck pond in 1171. The most important historical achievement of Martin's goose up until the present day happened shortly thereafter. The town of Jaffa, or Joppa, in Palestine was besieged by Muslim Saracens on St. Martin's Day in the year 1179. There were French crusaders in the town who bravely defended the castle from the pagans, however they had no intention of missing

the celebration of their St. Martin's feast day. They celebrated the holiday so wholeheartedly that the enemies, who were well aware of the Christian calendar of saints and its consequences, stormed Jaffa and were able to raise the Islamic flag over the towers and turrets without hardly ever having to use their swords.

St Martin's Goose Comes to Scandinavia

The feast day of St. Martin spread from France to Germany during medieval times, and during the Renaissance it was the Germans who saw to it that the celebration of the feast of St. Martin was spread to Scandinavia. The Danes, and with them the inhabitants of the now Swedish province of Skåne were the first ones to adopt this new autumn feast, which they did at the end of the 15th century.

It did not take long for the Swedes to accept the consumption of goose on St. Martin's Day. The first evidence of this is from 1557. It was primarily the kitchens of castles and manor houses that were equipped with spits on which a whole goose could be roasted. City folks could even leave their goose to be cooked in the ovens of the town bakeries by using the residual heat left after bread baking was done. But what about the farmers? Well, they would actually treat their slaughtered goose just like any other slaughtered meat: they would dress it and cure it with salt. Then they would take what was needed from their storeroom and cook the goose meat, which resulted in the other way of preparing goose in Sweden, a variant of goose confit, where the salted meat was cooked in its own fat. This dish, served with horseradish sauce, could be eaten at any time during the year. Goose is an excellent example of how social factors can result in variations in culinary methods.

It was not until the mid-1800s that farmers in Skåne in southern Sweden began to eat roast goose on St. Martin's Day.

Goose Delicacies From Other Provinces

Strangely enough, the "classic Skåne" goose menu, which begins with black soup (*svartsoppa*) and ends with either apple cake (*äpplekaka*) or a kind of pyramid cake baked on a spit, called a *spettekaka* in Swedish, was created in the early 1850s by the restaurant Piperska Muren, across the street from the City Hall in Stockholm. The traditional black soup was eaten in the early 16th century by people such as Bishop "Lappen" Brask in Linköping, and the oldest known recipe for what is known as Skåne apple cake, made from bread crumbs and applesauce, came from Cajsa Warg, a famous housekeeper and cookbook author from the town of Örebro in the mid-1700s. To this can be added that the famous *spettekaka* began its Swedish travels in Stockholm in the 1600s, having emigrated from the Baltic countries or possibly from Germany.

After all of these historical disclosures, I will probably have to put on a fake beard as a disguise before I ever dare to venture back into the gastronomic territory of Skåne.

Spettekaka, a kind of pyramid cake baked on a spit.

Advent

Advent

4 Sundays Before Christmas

Of the four Sundays of Advent, it is really only the first Sunday which is generally observed by most people. After that, the Christmas decorations in the department store windows attract larger audiences.

Curiously enough, Advent – the Latin word for arrival, implying the arrival of Christ – is actually older than Christmas itself strictly speaking, at least when we refer to Advent fasting in the Catholic Church. Already before the decision was made to celebrate the birth of Christ on December 25, there was a period of Epiphany fasting in both the eastern and the western churches, that is a fast in preparation for the celebration of the baptism of Jesus and his appearance as the son of God on the feast of the Epiphany on January 6 (called *Trettondagen* on the modern Swedish calendar, or the 13th day of Christmas). This period of fasting was already known in the 4th century. However in the western church during the 5th and 6th centuries increased interest in Christmas Day resulted in its replacing the Epiphany, and the Epiphany Fast was moved to the weeks before Christmas. This was stipulated in the year 480, and after some vacillation the Advent Fast and our present-day four week period of Advent were established.

Later it seems that Advent or Christmas fasting was shortened even more, and in Sweden today it at sunrise on December 13, the feast day of St. Lucia, and this contributed to the practice of serving spectacular breakfasts on this day.

Swedish Advent Celebrations

As a religious practice, Advent plays a very subordinate role in older Swedish folk traditions. Thus it is with holidays as it is with so much else: their popularity rises and wanes with no real explanation as to why this is so. Interest in observing Advent was minimal at the beginning of the 20th century. However this changed as the century progressed, and from the 1920s onwards the first Sunday of Advent became one of the major church-going days of the year. In some cities it is actually the most important day.

Swedish theologians have reflected a great deal upon why the celebration of Advent has become so popular, and they have not been very willing to accept the fact that this is due to our general tendency to jump the gun on Christmas celebrations, or the fact that in many places the First Sunday of Advent is also the premier showing of the Christmas window displays at the department stores. However these events certainly have contributed to this situation! When Swedes abandoned their subsistence economy where people produced everything they needed on their own farms, and changed over to a monetary economic system, the result was that the old way of preparing for Christmas together with other farms was replaced by purchases made from general stores and shops. People certainly have every right to speak disparagingly about the commercialization of Christmas. Yet no one can deny that the department store windows and the street decorations undoubtedly provide these December weeks with a festive atmosphere, and in this respect one should also consider Advent's special characteristic as a harbinger of the joyful and long-awaited Christmas celebration.

Advent Candles, Advent Trees, Advent Wreathes

Sometime during the 1870s, the lay workers at the children's home in Ersta, outside of Stockholm, assembled all of the children at dusk for a small ceremony in the church on the First Sunday of Advent. Seven of the children were allowed to walk up to a fir tree in the sanctuary and they each got to light a candle on the tree. During the service on the next Sunday the first seven candles were already lit and seven more children got to light seven new candles. This was repeated on the Third and Fourth Sundays of Advent.

The lay workers had thereby introduced the Advent tree, a new holiday tradition in Sweden which would appear in many different variations as time went on. It has been proven conclusively that the idea came from Germany because the initiators recounted that they had gotten the idea from Kaiserswerth, their sister organization in Düsseldorf.

The times were ripe for this idea in the 1870s since putting up and decorating Christmas trees prior to the Christmas holidays had become more popular in churches, barracks, old folks' homes and schools, etc. However the idea of adding another candle for each day of Advent was a new import.

Today Swedes are most familiar with the four Advent candles in a candleholder, which belongs to the same tradition whether they are burning in a home, on an altar, in a classroom or on a TV screen. Yet it is not possible to make a direct link between the modern tradition and the older one. The first person to describe the use of the four Advent candles was the archbishop Nathan Söderblom in 1896. His daughter, who in time became the wife of Archbishop Brilioth, had also related that this tradition had been practiced in her parents' home, and she added that they used to put candles on a juniper bush, something that is even a bit closer to the Advent trees in Ersta which the archbishop ought to have been familiar with.

An Advent wreath is another way to arrange Advent candles, a ring with four candles which is covered with evergreens. It also came from Germany where it was very popular during the 1920s and 1930s, mainly in cities. Certainly the Advent trees are the most original of these related customs, and they have been simplified so that only one candle is lit each Sunday instead of the 28 candles which earlier burned on the Advent tree on the fourth Sunday of Advent.

The Advent Calendar

The story of the Advent calendar began sometime around the end of the 19th century when Gerhard Lang, a little German boy, continually asked his mother how long it was until Christmas Eve. She came up with the idea of baking 24 cookies on December 1. She placed them on a piece of paper upon which she had written the numbers 1-24. Gerhard could then eat one cookie each day and thus easily count how many cookies, as well as days, that remained.

Eventually Gerhard became a businessman and one day he remembered his mother's ingenious idea of how to avoid children's nagging in December. He assumed that other mothers found themselves in the same predicament and realized that this ought to be something which could be profitable. So around

The first Advent calendar was designed by Aina Stenberg-Masolle, and it appeared in 1932. She continued to design Advent calendars up until 1964.

24
23
20
17
18
13
6
4
5
16
1
2
3
10

1920 he constructed the first Advent calendar which was comprised of 2 pieces of paper, one with pictures to cut out and one with numbered spaces where the pictures were to be glued. This was a huge unexpected success, and he soon designed a better model that had windows with pictures behind them, which we are most familiar with today. Finally the most financially successful variant appeared, the three-dimensional calendar, where you could place things behind the windows and thus charge a higher price. Eventually his calendars had such strange and complicated mechanisms that people thought they were too expensive and stopped buying them, so Herr Lang eventually went bankrupt. By then Advent calendars were a generally accepted Christmas item which soon would conquer the entire world.

I would now like to introduce you to Henny Strömman. She had learned about the custom of Advent calendars in Germany, and when she became the director of the Swedish Girl Scouts it occurred to her that Sweden did not have such playthings. So she approached the artist Aina Stenberg-MasOlle, famous for hundreds of Christmas cards, and who was said to have depicted her own farm in the province of Dalarna on the first Swedish Advent calendar. It was published for Christmas in 1932 in an edition of 10,000 copies. They disappeared so quickly that the artist would continue making calendars every year until 1964. By then the calendars were well established in Sweden and the Girl Scouts had competition. The greatest competition came from the Swedish Radio when they decided to link the calendar to a radio program in 1957. In 1961 Swedish TV was ready to copy the radio idea, and as a measure of their success it can be noted that 360,000 calendars were sold already in 1962. Even though Advent is certainly a religious concept, these TV calendars became more profane, and in 1972 the Swedish TV changed the name of the program from *The Advent Calendar* (*Adventskalendern*) to *The Christmas Calendar* (*Julkalendern*).

The Advent Star

In the 1800s there was a boarding school for the children of missionaries in Sachsen, Germany where a teacher came up with the idea of working with the students to make a kind of paper star with a place for a light inside. These were to be used to decorate the school during Advent.

In the city of Herrnhut there was a proprietor of a book and stationary store for missionaries who happened to see these impressive stars at the castle and he realized their commercial potential. Using them as a prototype which could be assembled, he constructed a star with detachable points making it easier to distribute and to store away after Christmas. The light source was a small kerosene or oil lamp which was later replaced by a light bulb. It turned out that the star, called a Moravian star, was very easily sold, and through the bookstore's efforts it developed into a cottage industry and soon their stars were available to customers far from the Herrnhut district.

After World War I the son of the bookstore owner created a new kind of star that could be folded together so that it hardly took any space. While the older star was more three-dimensional and usually had been placed under a chandelier or in a doorway, the new star could be hung in a window so that it would shine towards the street as well as inwards into the room. This actually was connected to an old urban tradition, namely to decorate windows toward the street with burning candles on Christmas morning as a greeting to all of the early morning churchgoers – comparable to the modern ramps of pyramid shaped lights that are used for the same purpose today! This turned out to be a stroke of luck. A veritable Advent star factory developed in Herrnhut, and in the 1930s they began exporting their stars to other countries, including Sweden.

The earliest Advent stars reached our country already before World War I by means of personal contacts between Swedish families, particularly those with links to the church and

to Germans living in the neighborhood of Herrnhut. In 1934 Swedish stationary wholesalers imported the first stars from Germany and they were sold in a flash. The German stars were rather expensive and in 1941 Erling Persson, who was later to found the huge clothing chain of Hennes & Mauritz, realized the inherent potential of the paper stars and he started producing them for the Swedish market together with his partner Björn Wennberg. They began by making Advent stars modeled after the German version. However in 1944 they hit upon a much cheaper, collapsible star that was a great success. The first year hundreds of thousands of stars were sold and suddenly Winter Sweden acquired a new appearance. From practically every window in the large apartment buildings there were flaming red stars shining from the first day of Advent, and these cheap decorations became so very popular that people in more snobbish circles, who followed the older traditions, disdainfully called them "proletarian stars." Undoubtedly it was a natural assumption to see a relationship between these red stars, which were not very different from the stars in the national symbols of the communist countries, and the political radicalization that came about in Sweden at the end of World War II. However a more down-to-earth explanation of their success was more probably the shortage of candles during the war years – the soft glow of the Advent stars provided something of the same Christmas atmosphere in households.

By the mid-1950s enthusiasm for the red stars began to wane, and later they were replaced to a great degree by more sophisticated models and much more expensive constructions made out of thin wooden strips, straw or copper. They offered more exciting effects and did not seem quite as banal. In recent years Christmas candleholders, both the five or eight pointed stars and the pyramid shaped ones, have been very successful items. Almost one million candleholders and about 300,000 stars of all kinds (and the exports were considerably higher) were sold during an ordinary Christmas in the 1990s, and this is in a country with a population of 9 million inhabitants.

Advent wreaths illuminate Swedish homes all throughout December.

Swedish Ginger Snaps

Pepparkakor

Swedish ginger snaps (or *pepparkakor)* are a must when celebrating Lucia or Christmas in Sweden. Here is an old family recipe with lots of spices (but no pepper).

1 ROUNDED CUP (250 ML) SUGAR
2/3 CUP (150 ML) MOLASSES
2 1/2 TEASPOONS CINNAMON
2 1/2 TEASPOONS GROUND CLOVES
2 1/2 TEASPOONS GINGER
3/4 TABLESPOON BICARBONATE OF SODA
1 CUP + 2 TEASPOONS (250 GRAMS) BUTTER
1 EGG
ABOUT 4 1/2 CUPS (1100 ML) FLOUR

Dissolve the sugar, molasses and spices in a saucepan. Remove from heat. Dissolve the bicarbonate of soda in a very small amount of water and add slowly while stirring. Melt the butter and add to the mixture. Beat the egg and add it, stirring well.

Pour the mixture into a bowl and add the flour (save a small amount for rolling out the dough). Refrigerate the dough overnight. It will become quite hard in the refrigerator, so take the dough out to temper it before rolling it out.

Knead the dough, a little bit at a time. Roll it out very thin with a rolling pin on a floured surface. Cut out shapes using cookie cutters.

Bake the cookies at 400° F. (200° C.) for 4-5 minutes. Watch them carefully, thin cookies burn easily. Store them in a cookie tin when they are cool.

Swedish Glögg

Glögg

Swedes drink warm glögg during the winter when it is cold and snowy outside. There are many different recipes. Here is an old family recipe which should be enjoyed in small portions.

1 BOTTLE OR CAN OF BEER
3 DRIED FIGS, EACH CUT INTO 4 PIECES
10 WHOLE CARDAMOM OR 20 CARDAMOM SEEDS
3 PIECES OF DRIED SEVILLE ORANGE PEEL
6 WHOLE CLOVES (OR MORE FOR THOSE WHO LIKE THEIR FLAVOR)
1 STICK CINNAMON
1 PIECE OF FRESH GINGER
1¼ CUPS (300 ML) SUGAR
1½ CUPS (37.5 CL) VODKA
3 CUPS (75 CL) MADEIRA
5 OUNCES (150 GRAMS) SMALL RAISINS
20 BLANCHED ALMONDS

Boil the beer with the spices in a saucepan and let simmer for 15 minutes. Add sugar and cook until everything is dissolved.

Let this mixture cool and add the vodka. Place the saucepan over a low heat and warm the mixture to 131° F. (55° C.). Heating it to a higher temperature will cause the alcohol to evaporate.

Allow this to stand and steep for 1 hour, after which the Madeira is added. The mixture should then continue to steep for another hour. Strain the liquid and pour it into a bottle.

To serve, heat the glögg to maximum 131° F. (55° C.) – heating it to a higher temperature is obviously a waste of God's good gifts. Serve in small cups with the almonds and raisins and a spoon.

Lucia Buns

Lussebullar

When Swedes long for Lucia, they also crave Lucia buns. They are absolutely essential for the Lucia celebration. This is the only time of the year when saffron is added to bread.

1 PACKAGE (50 GRAMS) YEAST
10½ TABLESPOONS (150 GRAMS) BUTTER
2 CUPS (500 ML) MILK
2 PACKETS (1 GRAM) SAFFRON
SCANT ½ CUP (100 ML) SUGAR
½ TEASPOON SALT
ABOUT 7 CUPS (1 KILOGRAM) FLOUR
RAISINS

Break the cake of yeast into small pieces in a bowl. Melt the butter, add milk and heat to 99° F. (37° C.). Pour liquid over yeast and stir to dissolve.

Add the saffron, sugar, salt and almost all of the flour (save a little bit for shaping the buns). Knead and let rise covered for about 40 minutes.

Heat the oven to 475° F. (250° C.). Place the dough on a floured surface and knead gently. Divide the dough into smaller pieces and roll each one into a "snake," which can then be formed into small s-shaped buns.

Place the buns on a baking sheet. Press a raisin into the indentation at both ends of each bun. Cover and let buns rise 10–15 minutes. Brush buns with a lightly beaten egg. Bake for 8–10 minutes. Allow them to cool under a clean towel.

Lucia

Lucia

December 13 is devoted to the martyr Lucia, a Christian virgin who lived in Syracuse in the third century. The Swedish Lucia celebration of today has very little to do with Italy however. During the 19th century the feast of Lucia was primarily held in homes as a celebration of light. The major public breakthrough for Lucia occurred in 1927 when a newspaper arranged a Lucia procession through Stockholm. Today we have Lucia processions in schools, at old people's homes and hospitals, etc., but there is no Lucia celebration in Italy.

Lucia has been celebrated in manor houses as a legendary saint ever since the mid 18th century, at least in western Sweden. Yet at the same time there also existed the older connection of her name to the devil Lucifer, particularly among country folk. In our own times she has become Swedish folklore's only export product – or rather, re-exported product.

Santa Lucia

December 13 is the feast day of the martyr Lucia on the calendar of saints. She was a Christian virgin who lived in Syracuse on the island of Sicily at the end of the 3rd century, and she was engaged to a pagan. In the year 304 she persuaded her mother to pay her dowry to her, which she immediately gave away to the poor. Her fiancé did not approve of the idea and he accused her of being a Christian, which led to her being sentenced to a brothel. When the time came to take her there she was frozen fast and could not be moved. A bonfire was built around her, but it burned without singeing a hair on her head. The executioner was then sent for, and he beheaded her. There is one vertebra from her neck which has actually been chopped in half in a church in Venice. However when it comes down to it, this girl's relics and her legend are completely unrelated to the Scandinavian Lucia – the only thing that she and

the saint have in common is their feast day on the calendar. So where does she really come from?

The Lucia dressed in white is a protestant replacement of St. Nicholas, the Catholic children's patron saint whose feast day on the calendar was December 6. On that day a grown-up came to school dressed as a bishop and he gave wheat buns and other goodies to the good children, while the devil, dressed in horns and fur, spanked the lazy, disobedient children with a switch. Of course Nicholas became a stumbling block for the Lutheran priests because saints were like salt in a wound to them.

In order to get rid of the children's saint, a new custom began where the Christ Child was the central figure. He was respectable enough to be the giver of gifts, even for evangelical priests, and they moved the entire Christmas event into people's homes, so that all of the links to Nicholas disappeared. Instead there was a girl who appeared in protestant western German homes at Christmas. She was dressed in a white gown and had a "halo" on her head in the form of a crown of candles. She was known as *Christkindlein* or *Kindchen* Jesus, or *Kinken Jes* in Low German, and she gave presents to good children. The old devil from the Nicholas scenario was still viable in both the evangelical and the Catholic teachings, so he was allowed to remain. When we call Lucia's saffron buns for *lussekatter* in Swedish today, it is a reminder of the devil in older Swedish traditions because back then they were called *dövels-katter*, or devil's cats.

Lucia Becomes a Success

The *Kinken Jes* was brought to Sweden by the Germans towards the end of the 17th century, but they never succeeded in transplanting this into Swedish Christmas celebrations – the strict "orthodox" priests surely thought that such things were not suitable for such a serious celebration. The spectacular attire became associated with St. Lucia's Day during the 18th and 19th centuries in the manor houses around Lake Vänern.

This happened because the word "Lucia" is related to the word *Lux*, the Latin word for light. During the early 1800s western Swedes began to spread the Lucia tradition to places like universities, and at the same time it spread to farms in western Sweden as well.

Lucia did not make her public breakthrough until 1927 when a newspaper in Stockholm arranged a public Lucia procession through the city. Lucia's fate is a typical example of the labyrinthian path that a tradition can take, however it also shows the need in our times for a holiday that is not exclusively for the nuclear family, it suits other groups that have become important today – organizations, schools and old people's homes, just to name a few. Yet no one in Italy has ever seen a Lucia, and Italians are always very surprised when they realize just how successful their old saint has become in the Nordic regions.

It is nothing new that youngsters take the opportunity at Lucia to enjoy themselves (and to drink). These days they dress up with a bit of Christmas tree glitter in their hair and wear white lab coats with a pocket for a bottle (even though Walpurgis Eve has more often come to replace Lucia as a weekend for nocturnal carousing).

Lucia comes, bringing coffee, Saffron buns (lussebullar) and Swedish ginger snaps (pepparkakor).

TILL EMMY SOM ETT MINNE AF
UNGARNA I SUNDBORN. AF AUCTOR
C.L.
1892.

Christmas

Jul

It does not matter whether you are a Dane, a Norwegian or a Swede, an Icelander or a Faroe Islander, they all use the same word for Christmas, *jul* or *jól*, which most people nowadays consider to be the most important holiday of the year.

It is generally accepted that the word *jul* has very ancient Germanic roots. When the Anglo-Saxons invaded England in the 5th and 6th centuries, they brought this Germanic word with them, and the words Yule and Yuletide still exist, particularly in northern English dialects. In other languages the word for Christmas usually has some relationship to the birth of Jesus (e.g. *noël* in French) or some variation on the word Christ Mass (e.g. *Christmas* in English). Early missionaries tried to introduce the latter term into the Nordic languages, though without much luck. However they were more successful in England, and the German word *Weihnacht* or Holy Night clearly has a Christian meaning as well.

Pre-Christian Yuletide and Labor Festivals

Perhaps the pre-Christian yuletide was a labor related festival to celebrate the end of the harvest or the main autumn slaughtering, which of course offered the possibility of exces-

The Day Before Christmas Eve (Dagen före Julafton) is what Carl Larsson called this painting from Sundborn in Dalarna, 1892.

A Nordic Christmas tree painted by Jenny Nyström around 1890. She was the mother of the Swedish Santa Claus (jultomten).

sive amounts of food to accompany beer drinking. To "Drink Yule" is an expression that was first noted around the year 900 (in connection with the Norwegian king Harald Hårfagre). This concept later became a part of Nordic Christmas celebrations over the centuries.

We know that during Viking times our pagan Nordic forefathers celebrated several feasts connected to offerings or *blot* (for example the Elven Sacrifice or *alvablot*) during the months closest to the turn of the year, although it is not possible to point to any particular celebration that happened at the same time as our Christian Christmas. However it is quite certain that the term *jul* originated from some of these festivals or celebration periods.

The switch in Sweden from the Catholic church to the Lutheran church during the 16th century had no particularly dramatic effects on Swedish Christmas celebrations. Among other things we can find reminders of the Christmas Fast which began on Lucia morning during the Middle Ages and lasted until midnight on Christmas Eve. *Lutfisk* or *lutefisk,* as it often is known in English speaking countries (dried cod or ling which is soaked in water and lye before cooking), is the best example of this. This typically medieval dish, which was served during periods of fasting, is still eaten by 25% of the Swedish population as a part of Christmas dinner.

The Christmas Crèche

Among Lutherans the Christmas crèche was long considered to be a Catholic idea, and it was not until 1803 that such a controversial thing could be shown publically in Stockholm. The very first crèche was arranged on Christmas day in 1223 in an Italian village by none other than St. Francis of Assisi himself, who held a mass in a cave where a live ox and an equally authentic donkey served as extras. The original crèche from Bethlehem, a genuine venerated relic, is much older, and the five decaying (beech wood) boards that are presently mounted in a casing of silver and crystal, have been on display since the 4th century in the Church of Santa Maria Maggiore in Rome.

It was not until 1929 that a Swedish parish priest in Malmö took the bold step of setting up a Christmas crèche in his church. This courageous pioneer had to undergo a great deal of criticism from traditionalist colleagues and parishioners, yet one church in Stockholm was quickly ready to follow suite, and during the 1930s the custom of Christmas crèches spread throughout the country. Whatever one may think about their kitschy design – the crèches are the only thing left in our Christmas celebrations that remind us of the constantly fading religious background of Christmas.

Christmas cards were popular motifs for many Swedish illustrators.

The Christmas Tree

The indoor Christmas tree has its roots in southwestern Germany and Switzerland, where it was mentioned around the end of the Middle Ages. It was thanks to Martin Luther that it first spread throughout much of Europe. He wanted holidays to be celebrated at home rather than with processions through the streets. The Christmas tree fit well into this concept and Protestantism had to tolerate being called "the Christmas tree religion" by Catholics (who built Christmas crèches instead). In the beginning the trees were only decorated with apples and other sweets. The first person who described a tree decorated with candles was actually a Swedish officer who was wounded

at the Battle of Lützen and who spent Christmas of 1632 as a convalescent with a family in Leipzig. Some 100 years later the Countess Wrede-Sparre related the story of the first Christmas tree known in Sweden, and for a long time this exclusive item was primarily a distinctly upper-class luxury. Up until the mid-1800s they were usually only small trees that were placed on tables, but later the ceiling-high trees became popular in the 1850s. The last phase of Christmas tree history are the outdoor Christmas trees decorated with lights – both private ones and municipal ones – which became popular during the 1930s.

The Swedish Santa Claus, Jultomten

The Swedish Santa Claus, *Jultomten,* looks his actual age as he waddles around in his old fashioned clothes and his unkempt beard. Our Santa Claus in the form of *Jultomten* is a curious bastardization, originating from a combination of the Catholic St. Nicolas and the supernatural elves and brownies who were the farm guardians in Nordic folklore. They were known as *Nissar* (singular *nisse*) to Danes and Norwegians, and *tomtar* or *tomtegubbar* (singular *tomte* or *tomtegubbe*) to Swedes. For his almost explosive success, the *Jultomte* can thank the Swedish poet Viktor Rydberg for his pedagogical saga, *Little Vigg's Adventures on Christmas Eve,* and his philosophical poem "*Tomten*" (written in 1881), as well as Jenny Nyström's never-ending flow of *tomte* portraits. By a stroke of luck, Rydberg's and Nyström's interest in *tomtar* and elves occurred at the same time as the great upswing in Christmas buying sprees during the month of December. These were stimulated by such novelties as department store windows and advertisements for Christmas presents. What brought about the demise of Nyström's elves was actually an American of Swedish descent, Haddon Sundblom, who in 1931 created the Coca Cola drinking "fat Santa" which most people consider to be our prototype of Santa Claus. The plump Coca Cola Santa's vocabulary is unfortunately rather limited, since he only seems to say, "Ho, ho, ho!".

The morning of Christmas Eve, 2010.

It was only about 100 years ago that Santa Claus (jultomten) marched into Swedish homes – so here in Sweden he looks his actual age. In Sweden and the other Nordic countries our jultomte distributes Christmas presents on Christmas Eve – December 24 – rather than on Christmas Day as is customary in many other countries.

Following pages: Carl Larsson's classic painting, Christmas Eve, A Christmas Table (Julafton, ett julbord) from 1904, shows how middle class people celebrated Christmas by trying to return to their roots.

What is unique about the Swedish Christmas elf or *tomte* is that he comes into the family circle with a bag of presents and utters his classic line, "Are there any good children here?," instead of the nocturnal visit where he comes down the chimney like in other countries.

Christmas Food

Why do Swedes celebrate the birth of their Savior with orgies in pork? Our Christmas smorgasbords (*smörgåsbord*) are weighted down with hams, head cheese, spare ribs, roasted hog's head coated with breadcrumbs and with an apple in its mouth, pork sausages and pig feet, yes, even pig tails in jelly. This was a result of the dominating role that pork played in meat production in the olden days, partly because of our forefathers' methods of conservation, pickling food in brine. During the big slaughter in October or November there was a mountain of pork to be dealt with, and the only possibility available for preserving it until the next slaughter one year later, was to salt it. This led to the almost constant chewing of more or less hard salted pork all year long. Usually there were one or two pigs that were saved to be slaughtered at Christmas. During a couple of Christmas weeks it was a real treat to be able to eat fresh meat without having to grit your teeth on salt crystals. During the course of the 1800s when the Swedish upper class created our contemporary Christmas traditions based on their understanding of what a genuine peasant Christmas was, pork stayed in place, riding high. Our food industry had continued to promote this, and naturally enough, seen to it that the "classic" Christmas menu has become a Swedish standard as well. Therefore 85% of Swedish homes serve Christmas ham, while the consumption of boiled ham during the rest of the year is rather insignificant. The dominance of pork is also very evident on the restaurants' sumptuous Christmas smorgasbords. By the way, did you know that in 2010 Swedes indulged themselves on Christmas food in restaurants for more than two billion Swedish crowns (about 226 million Euros or 301 million U.S. dollars)?

The Best of Everything at Christmastime

In pre-industrial peasant society, Christmas food basically included the best of everything there was to offer, according to the economic circumstances of the local district. What we today consider to be typical Christmas food was, once upon a time, food that was served by country folks at celebrations, whether it be a wedding, a funeral or a holiday. "Fancy folks" did not eat such things at Christmas – the Christmas dinner which a family in a manor house or a merchant would eat in the mid-1800s very rarely sank to the level where pork, *lutfisk* and porridge were standard dishes, and the image of Swedish people chewing on pork in unison is, in actual fact, rather recent.

In many homes there are quite a few very old local specialties that still exist. People in the south of Sweden still eat mustard sauce with their *lutfisk*, Stockholmers prefer to eat theirs with green peas or béchamel sauce (which nowadays has become the "national tradition" – otherwise it was most common to eat it with melted butter and pepper). The Christmas food issues of weekly magazines and daily newspapers, as well as the grocery stores' identical assortments of raw materials and prepared foods have greatly contributed to the standardization of the Christmas menu.

One would think that we ought to have begun to be influenced at least a little by the exciting and delicious Christmas dishes that immigrants have brought with them, however these cultural loans are few and far between thus far. More prevalent are emerging influences from certain foreign Christmas food customs that have been touted in the media, par-

Pickled Herring with Lemon

Inlagd sill med citron

Swedes eat herring whenever they can, usually on festive occasions such as Christmas, Easter and Midsummer, and even at other times just because they like it so much. It is best when eaten together with hard boiled eggs or potatoes.

5 HERRING FILLETS
1¼ CUPS (300 ML) SUGAR
JUICE OF 3 LARGE LEMONS
½ CUP WATER
1 LEEK
1 RED ONION
2 SMALL CARROTS
2 TABLESPOONS DILL
10 WHOLE ALLSPICE

Mix the sugar, lemon juice and water. Stir until the sugar has dissolved. Cut the herring fillets into bite sized pieces and add to the liquid mixture.

Slice the leek, onion and carrots in 1/8″ (3 mm) slices. Add to the herring mixture. Chop the dill, crush the allspice and add both ingredients to the herring.

Refrigerate for 2 days before serving.

Classic Swedish Meatballs

Klassiska köttbullar

Meatballs are traditionally a standard feature on the Swedish Christmas table, the smörgåsbord. However meatballs are eaten all through the year. They are usually served with the classic accompaniments of mashed potatoes, gravy and lingonberries.

Serves 4, 30–40 meatballs

SCANT ½ CUP (100 ML) MILK
BREADCRUMBS
1 TEASPOON SALT
WHITE PEPPER
½ ONION
½ POUND (200 GRAMS) GROUND PORK
¾ POUND (300 GRAMS) GROUND BEEF
1 EGG

Mix the milk and breadcrumbs in a bowl, add salt and pepper and allow breadcrumbs to swell. Peel and finely chop the onion. Blend all of the ingredients into a smooth mixture.

Roll tablespoonfuls of the mixture into small round balls. Melt butter in a large frying pan over medium high heat. Add some of the meatballs, do not crowd them, and sauté them quickly. Reduce heat and continue sautéing them until the meatballs are completely done.

Jansson's Temptation

Janssons frestelse

There is never a Christmas smörgåsbord (or a traditional buffet) without Jansson's Temptation! This dish is often eaten very late at night as a light supper dish, for example late on New Year's Eve. The name of the dish comes from a 1928 film with the same name.

Serves 4

2 ONIONS
8 POTATOES
4½ OUNCES (1 CAN, ABOUT 125 GRAMS) SWEDISH ANCHOVY FILLETS (which actually are pickled sprats). Mediterranean anchovies may be used sparingly instead, though beware, they are much saltier!)
1¼ CUPS (300 ML) CREAM
JUICE FROM THE ANCHOVIES
¼ CUP (50 ML) BREAD CRUMBS
2 TABLESPOONS BUTTER

Turn oven on to 425° F (225° C). Peel the onion and slice very thinly. Peel the potatoes and cut them into thin matchstick sized strips. Layer the potatoes, the onion slices and the Swedish anchovies alternately in a well-greased ovenproof pan. End with a layer of potatoes on top. Pour the cream over the casserole and add some of the juice from the anchovies. Sprinkle with fine bread crumbs and dot with pats of butter. Bake until the potatoes are done and are golden brown, about 45-60 minutes.

Dark Rye Bread

Kavring

Swedes enjoy eating dark bread. Here is a recipe for a classic loaf of rye soda bread that goes well with Christmas ham or pickled herring at Midsummer.

Serves 4

1½ CUPS (400 ML) MOLASSES
2½ TABLESPOONS BICARBONATE OF SODA
1½ CUPS + 1 TABLESPOON (400 ML) FLOUR
3 C. + 2 TABLESPOONS (800 ML) RYE FLOUR MIXTURE (40-50% sifted rye flour + 50-60% wheat flour, called rågsikt in Swedish)
1 TABLESPOON SALT
2½ CUPS (600 ML) BUTTERMILK

Set oven at 350° F. (180° C.). Oil two rectangular loaf pans (1½ quarts). Dust oiled surface with flour or breadcrumbs. Mix all of the dry ingredients in a bowl. Add buttermilk and molasses. Stir quickly into a dough. Distribute the dough in the two loaf pans. Bake in the lower half of the oven for about 60 minutes.

The early morning church service on Christmas day (jul-ottan) has become something of a symbol for the Swedish Christmas celebration. When a Swedish Christmas is depicted for a foreign audience in a film or on TV, one of the high-lights is the exotic ride

ticularly Anglo-Saxon ones such as plum pudding and turkey. Yet it is unusual that they are allowed to replace the Swedish Christmas menu here, rather they sneak onto dinner tables and into parties during the week between Christmas and New Year's.

Christmas Day – The Birthday of Christ?

If you take out your Bible and begin searching, you will not find there the slightest indication of the actual season of the year when the remarkable birth of the infant Jesus took place,

nor will you find a date. One clue, the information about the shepherds, reveals that this event could hardly have occurred in the midst of midwinter. They never would have spent a night outside at the end of December – nights at that time of year are very cold in the area around Bethlehem.

in a horse-drawn sleigh in the light of burning torches. However today the early morning service has been replaced by Christmas prayers (julbön) and midnight mass (midnattsmässa).

When Jesus Was Given A Birthday

No, the choice of December 25 was based upon religion and political realism. In the Roman Empire at the beginning of our era there were several redemption theories which were vying

to become the official religion of the Roman state. Most successful during the 3nd century was the Mithras cult from the Near East, a kind of macho-oriented sun worship interspersed with elements of an imperial cult (the Evangelists, in particular Matthew, borrowed a great deal from their mythology). For this reason it was favored by several Roman emperors who established December 25 as the major feast day of this imperial cult, making it a very special day with equal amounts of political and religious significance.

The Early Christian leaders were very pragmatic – results were more important than ideology. They understood that Christianizing people would be difficult if they were not allowed to continue following their celebrations and traditions, so they let people keep their old customs. Instead they gave these celebrations a respectable Christian appearance. In 354 Pope Liberius decreed that from that point on Jesus Christ was officially born on December 25. The Emperor Theodosius the Great made Christianity the national religion in the 380s. However after his death the Roman Empire was divided into an eastern and a western empire. In the eastern empire, with its center in Constantinople, people were not very interested in what the Pope devised. So while December 25 became the birthday of Jesus in the western empire under the rule of Rome, the eastern churches continued to follow an older tradition (which had its roots in Egypt) where January 6 was celebrated as the commemoration of the baptism of Jesus, or rather his spiritual birth, and this is still the custom there today.

Though it is not really relevant here, it is worth pointing out that even the year Jesus was born – and thus the starting point of our entire chronology – is a barely credible guess made by an English monk more than 700 years after the fact. We now know that the terrible Jewish king Herod died in the year 4 B.C., and therefore could hardly have ordered the infant murders which were supposed to have taken place shortly after the birth of Jesus.

"Tomten," the famous classic Christmas poem in Sweden, begins with the line: "The cold of the midwinter night is severe" (Midvinternattens köld är hard). It was written by the author Viktor Rydberg during a winter stroll in 1881. The poem was illustrated by Jenny Nyström.

Midvinternattens köld är hård,
stjernorna gnistra och glimma.
Alla sofva i enslig gård
djupt under midnattstimma.
Månen vandrar sin tysta ban,
snön lyser hvit på fur och gran,
snön lyser hvit på taken.
Endast tomten är vaken,

Står der så grå vid lad'gårdsdörr,
grå vid den hvita drifva,
tittar, som många vintrar förr,
upp emot månens skifva,
tittar mot skogen, der gran och fur
drar kring gården sin dunkla mur,
grubblar, fast ej det lär båta,
öfver en underlig gåta,

New Year's Day

Nyår

Of course we usually think that knowing when New Year's Day occurs is definitely not a problem. No, it is not for us westerners today. However if you ask a Chinese, a Vietnamese, a Jewish or a Muslim person the same question you would get four different suggestions. And however well thought out our calendar seems to be – why ever is the ninth month named September since that word means seven? Why does February only have 28 days, and why does the extra day in a leap year come at the end of February and not in December, which certainly would be more logical?

Celebrate New Year's Day in March?

Well, in ancient Rome it was the first of March which was New Year's Day up until 153 B.C. – which explains why the extra day in a leap year falls when it does and why the ninth month is called the seventh month! In Rome New Year's Day was the day when the consuls, the highest government officials of the city and the state, assumed office. During the era of the Roman Republic (about 90 B.C.) they were also the military commanders in chief. The Roman men used to spend their summers fighting the annual war. This date worked well as long as Rome was a small city state, however when the empire and the army expanded, the new consuls did not have enough time to

Following pages: A winter day in the village of Övre Gårdsjö in Dalarna, Pettersgården.

train the soldiers after the first of March. So the date for changing consuls, and thus for beginning the New Year, were both moved to January 1 – however the old names of the months were difficult to change, so they have remained the same to this day.

The Romans celebrated January 1 with huge celebrations, and for this reason the Early Christian church was not particularly interested in keeping this date. So the beginning of the ecclesiastical year was moved to Christmas Day, which in Sweden was considered to be New Year's Day all the way up until the 16th century when the continental practice of printing calendars was adopted and Sweden returned to the classic order.

New Year's Day Then and Now

Many people celebrate the evening of New Year's Eve in restaurants and even more celebrate at home in the company of friends and acquaintances in a more or less elitist upper class manner. Champagne or simpler sparkling wine corks are popped in restaurants, in neighborhoods with row houses and single family homes, and on high-rise balconies while fireworks and sparklers are set off, to the dismay of every dog owner around. Ham and porridge is forsaken for menus of lobster and beef tenderloin, and the streets are filled with gangs of young people who go from one bar to the next disco. In the midst of all of this exhilaration it is difficult to find anything that has its roots in the pre-industrial peasant culture that so greatly influenced Christmas food and beverages, the games and the entertainment.

How was New Year's Eve celebrated earlier, before restaurants and caterers took over? The answer of course depends upon which social echelon we happen to move within. Country folk marked the holiday mainly by eating more of the good Christmas food once again, and this is also what many families of the bourgeoisie did far into the 20th century. The habit of "waiting up" for the stroke of midnight was quite unknown

among farmers, although it did happen that young people gathered at the church and snuck up into the bell tower without permission so they could "ring in" the new year at midnight while yelling and screaming. If there were no church bells then you could also "shoot in" the new year with a gun, a custom (or a bad habit) that is related to the more spectacular fireworks of today. The synchronized ringing of church bells at midnight on New Year's Eve only became customary after World War I.

In Sweden perhaps the most noted practice was to "curtsey for the New One of the New Year," that is for the first new moon of the new year. Unmarried young women who wished to learn their destiny were supposed to go out into the night alone, curtsey three times for the new moon and then open the Bible or psalm book which they had with them to a random page. It would be possible to deduce their future from the text on the page which fell open. These kinds of fortune telling and predictions have disappeared in our more rational times, although we have adopted a replacement of sorts from the continent, the new tradition of making New Year's resolutions. In opposition to the formal Bragi Promise of the Viking era which was made during the ceremony known as Christmas Drinking, our New Year's resolutions are usually made in secret. It somehow seems safer that way.

That which definitely inserted the New Year's Eve vigil into Swedish family life was the radio, which began broadcasting serious official New Year's programs. Later on the radio was surpassed by television's more entertainment oriented New Year's celebrations, although in both cases Tennyson's "Ring Out, Wild Bells" was recited as a commemorative culmination.

The New Year's fireworks at Skansen attract large crowds of people and the event is broadcast live on Swedish TV. Alfred Tennyson's poem, "Ring Out, Wild Bells," is recited, which has been a tradition since 1895.

FYRVERKERI PÅ
SKANSEN

The Epiphany

Trettondag jul

January 13

True, Swedes think that it is Knut who shoos Christmas away, but they, the Finland-Swedes (and some Finns) together with the Norwegians are the only ones who do. The Epiphany is universally accepted as the last "true" day of the Christmas holidays because St. Knut's Day has never become a red letter day on any calendars. This is when Christmas food began to run out and people had to be satisfied with scraping the last bits from the hambone and the spare ribs, which resulted in this holiday being called bone shaking day (*benraskedagen*).

Priests prefer to use the pre-Christian name Epiphany, *epifania* in Greek, which comes from a verb meaning to be manifest, to appear. It was so named because in the oldest early church the memory of the appearance of Christ to the world was celebrated on that day, when St. John the Baptist baptized him and his short career as a prophet began. This interpretation has lived on in the eastern churches.

Three Wise Men

When the western churches agreed that Jesus was born on Christmas day, December 25, they also linked the Epiphany to the Christmas celebration and gave it new content, namely to commemorate the visit to the stall in Bethlehem of the three Wise Men, Caspar, Melchior and Balthazar. Over time the Magi, advanced to the rank of the Three Holy Kings.

Since three kings in a row are quite unusual, even in the circles of saints, these three Eastern potentates were perfect for embellishing the medieval mystery plays about the birth and childhood of Jesus. During the High Middle Ages, when the plays began to be performed even outside of the churches and often in the local languages, mainly in Italy, Germany and France, they became a source of inspiration for the Christmas plays that later on were developed in the protestant schools as well. They were also the inspiration for the singing processions of the Star Boys from the 17th century which were performed by young people in cities and villages in all of the Nordic countries as a feature at Christmas among the many begging pranks.

Staffan Singers

In Sweden students from high schools and other larger schools were the first to be given permission to go from house to house in an orderly fashion and sing their Christmas carols. Afterwards they could earn rather good pay from the audience. Later on they were allowed – up until the end of 1835 – to walk throughout the parish, or to *gå sockengång,* out in the countryside. Surely it was these walks through the parish that later on inspired youngsters in the villages to walk around as Star Boys or "Staffan Singers." There was probably an huge difference in the singing quality of these choirs, which could range from teacher directed choirs singing in harmony in the cities to the bellowing of the wandering Star Boys in the villages.

These days Star Boys, dressed in conical hats decorated with gold stars, have become a rather traditionless feature in the choirs and retinues of the Lucia processions. Sometimes these mixtures of traditions in the processions could attract even more attention by including the figure of a Christmas goat whose main role was to misbehave.

The three Wise Men.

St. Knut's Day

Tjugondag Knut

January 13

Of all of the medieval Danish kings there is mainly one whom Swedes know something about (at least his funny name), Sven Forked Beard or Sven Tveskägg as he is known in Sweden. He had a nephew, Sven Estridsen, who had 19 illegitimate children, of which five succeeded one another as king. Naturally this guaranteed an inflation of crown princes in the following generation. By the time that old King Sven's bundle of sons finally began to die off, his grandchildren realized that there were all too many cousins who could make a legitimate claim to the king's crown.

One of them was named Knut, a.k.a. Knut Lavard – "Lavard" being an aristocratic Danish title. Duke Knut was an ambitious youngster. Through cunning and bribes he gained title to the kingdom of the Slavic Obotrites in present day Mecklenburg, and thus attained a ranking that placed him in line to succeed his uncle Nils, the last in the line of brothers who were kings.

However Nils' son, Duke Magnus, began to plan for his own accession by doing away with Knut. Knut celebrated Christmas at his uncle's court in 1130 when Magnus planned to put his murder plans into action. He thought that it ought to be done in a neat and chivalrous way so he waited until the 20 days of Christmas were over, a period known as *julfrid* or Christmas Peace. On January 7, 1131, the day after the Epiphany (*Trettondagen* in Swedish), he lured his relative out into the secluded Haralsted Forest, drew his sword and clove Knut Lavard's skull with a mighty blow – to quote the legend:"From the left ear to the right eye so that his brains ran out." Neither his departure from this earthly life nor Knut's past seem to have merited a saint's halo. Yet one fine day his son Valdemar the Great became king of Denmark, and in 1169 he managed to get the Pope to include his father Knut on the golden ledger of saints, where his uncle's name, St. Knut, had been registered already in 1100.

During the Middle Ages the date of Knut's death, January 7,was given his name and so it has remained until today in Denmark. Also in Sweden that day was St. Knut's Day on the calendar until the end of the 17th century, but during the later part of that century it became more common for St. Knut's Day to be moved to January 13, and this became the rule from the 18th century.

Knut Shoos Christmas Away

It was probably so that people in some places had a time-honored belief that the Christmas holidays lasted for 20 days, while in other places they ended on the Epiphany, January 6. This is how the original St. Knut's Day became a red letter day since it was the first ordinary day after the holidays. The Swedish rhyme,"Knut shoos Christmas away" or *"Knut kör julen ut,"* originally belonged to the latter tradition and in old times it always had exactly that form. The other version of the rhyme, "Twenty Day Knut shoos Christmas away" or *"Tjugondag Knut kör julen ut,"* is more recent and first appeared during the 18th century. It is possible that Tjugondag Knut is a kind of contamination between both traditions at the end of Christmas, and it became established on the calendars in accordance with the more northern Scandinavian perception of the twentieth day of Christmas.

Knut the Swedish Way

The oldest account of the Swedish celebration on the twentieth day of Christmas can be found in Olof Rudbeck the Elder, who described something called a banquet war in his work *Atlantica* (1679-1702) where the guests were symbolically cast out. For the most part it can be said of our Knut traditions that they do not give the impression of being very old. Most of them are local and they often seem to parallel the things people did on other holidays.

The most widespread Knut tradition was to dress up as an old man Knut (*Knutsgubbe*). In some towns there are still children who dress up and paint their faces and then run around knocking on doors and asking to "sweep out Christmas."

What does belong to the twentieth day of Christmas tradition is of course taking down the Christmas tree (*julgransplundring*). The Christmas tree tradition and the edible Christmas tree decorations together with the Christmas tree plundering party arrived in Sweden from Germany during the 19th century. The Swedish term for Christmas tree plundering, *julgransplundring* was first seen in print in the magazine *Husmodern* in 1922, which is significant. This was the kind of weekly family magazine that came to shape this new addition to our Christmas celebrations.

Finally if we want take a look at the cream of society then it lies close at hand to point out the Knut dances, social events which remain prevalent in southern Swedish cities where there still are or have been Knut guilds since medieval times.

On January 13th Swedes "shoo Christmas away," usually together with their children who are allowed to "plunder" the Christmas tree. They have a little party where the Christmas tree is thrown out and everyone gets a small bag of candy to take home.

Valentine's Day

Alla hjärtans dag

February 14

In the mid-1980s a new "celebration day" became popular in Sweden, without any bells and whistles, but rather with bouquets of flowers, romantic cards, pastries decorated with hearts and heart shaped boxes filled with heart shaped red candies – for Valentine's Day. Already during the 1960s some clever shop owners had tried to launch the Anglo-Saxon tradition of Valentine's Day as the Swedish *Alla hjärtans dag* (All Hearts' Day). However at that point in time it was not very popular for Swedish hearts to adopt American commercial trends. In the early 1980s at least some florists managed to get their female customers interested in giving their women friends flower arrangements planted in heart shaped small porcelain pots. This idea quickly spread, with numerous branches of the gift industry showing pleasingly upward curves in their sales.

At the beginning of the 1990s Valentine's Day took an unexpected leap into a completely new milieu, namely the schools, where it became very popular to give a flower to someone to show that you liked them. A carnation usually shows "Friendship," while a rose symbolizes more passionate relationships. In some schools students choose between three different colored roses which they send to one another: yellow for friendship, pink for flirtation and red for love. Yet how did this ever begin? Well, it was definitely not in the U. S. A., which most people believe, but rather in classical Antiquity!

Bishop Valentine

Valentine was the name of the bishop in the city of Terni which lay north of Rome. He left this earthly existence on Via Flaminia, the major road leading north from this famous city. According to his official saint's legend, it was there, sometime around the year 270, that he was first killed by a pagan mob armed with sticks and clubs and then beheaded. Why this grim double fated destiny? Well, it seems that he apparently enraged people because of his success in converting new Christians. He was, among other things, imprisoned because of his Christian faith, and he preached so well that he was able to convert his prison guards to the new faith, and he then convinced them to free all of the imprisoned Christians and allow their families to be baptized. He was supposed to have performed various miracles as well, such as restoring the sight of a blind Christian princess – of course pagan mobs would have murdered for much less.

However there is another legend as well, where he apparently angered the emperor by sabotaging his attempts to press unmarried young men into service as conscripts during a war campaign. The young men were more inclined to cuddle with their sweethearts rather than going off to war. They began getting engaged and married at such a fast pace that there were soon no more unmarried young men eligible for military service left in Rome. So the emperor forbade all marriages. The good Bishop Valentine performed mass weddings in secret for young couples until Emperor Claudius got news of this and threw him into prison, and there he died on February 14. This version most certainly appeared much later as an explanation of why Valentine's Day became the day to give your sweetheart presents, and Valentine himself was transformed into the special patron saint for people in love, which definitely is something they need!

A Love Lottery

However a legend is not even necessary. In actual fact it is quite certain that a much earlier Roman tradition is the real origin of Valentine's Day. In ancient Rome February 15 was the date for a curious celebration called Lupercalia. Old people and young people celebrated the feast in different ways; here we will focus on the younger group.

It was said that during Lupercalia Roman youth could compete in a lottery for the fairest maidens in the city by choosing a piece of paper upon which they had written their names. This practice is undoubtedly quite similar to the much later English custom where pieces of paper with the names of the boys and the girls on them are put in two separate containers, after which each group takes turns drawing the name of someone of the opposite sex. Having done that, they were considered to be paired together as "Valentines" for the season, or even longer.

We can find the northernmost manifestation of this tradition with couples in Denmark, where the boy was called *gadebasse* in Danish (a street ram, or *gatubagge* in Swedish) and the girl was called *gadelamm* (a street ewe, or *gatulamm* in Swedish). After a long period of discussion, it was customary there to pair together those who seemed best suited for one another already on New Year's Eve, and it often happened that the street rams would keep their street ewes for the rest of their lives.

This tradition never managed to make its way to Sweden, although there are remnants of it in the province of Skåne in southern Sweden. Actual Valentine's Day celebrations may very likely be an Anglo-Saxon version of the recently discussed continental pastime for young people. During the 14th century the English poet Geoffrey Chaucer wrote that it was on Valentine's Day that the birds chose their mates for the summer, a statement that the designers of Valentine's Day cards took to heart during the 18th and 19th centuries: there are kissing finches everywhere in the amazing Valentine Museum in York.

In 1870 there were one million Valentine cards mailed in England. Sweden was not struck by Valentine's Day fever until after the Second World War.

"Survivals"

There was also another possibility, namely that the celebration of Valentine's Day is what we call a survival, that is a custom from the upper class that has continued on as a custom among country folks. One proof of a more developed celebration of Valentine's Day is the fact that Charles, the Duke of Orléans, wrote Valentine's Day ballads to his wife and other fair ladies-in-waiting during the 15th century. Here we approach the culture which showcased flirtation and the courting of the "queen of one's heart." I am alluding to medieval French courtly love, accompanied by yearning troubadours of course.

However the custom actually began, the celebration of Valentine's Day was a widespread aristocratic and bourgeois convention in 18th and 19th century England. There it became more popular during the 19th century, as did the greeting cards made to send on Valentine's Day, which were a precursor to Christmas cards. In 1820 the British Post Office delivered some 20,000 more letters on February 14 than otherwise, and 50 years later the numbers were over a million. Soon the custom was just as popular in the U. S. A., and it was actually strange that we in the Nordic countries managed to avoid this tradition until after World War II. Imported from Anglo-Saxon customs, gifts and greetings on Valentine's Day are now considered to be one of our most recent celebrations, to the delight of stationary stores, florists, gift shops and the post office.

And yet, is Valentine's Day delightful and advantageous for all hearts? No, certainly not. Especially within the framework of schools, this celebration is obviously not just a happy day for those who are chosen to receive flowers and candy, but also a time of wounded self-esteem and disappointment for those who are excluded. Thus older traditional celebrations often differ in this respect because everyone is included, in opposition to the newer celebrations which are only enjoyed by those who are popular, successful and attractive.

New Swedes, New Celebrations

During the 1930s Sweden was often described as one of the most homogeneous nations in Europe – in terms of ethnicity, language, religion and culture. The fact that there have come wave after wave of immigrants over the last thousand years and that we had an indigenous population up in the north did not change this idealized image of "Swedishness." This conformity is most noticeable in the area of religion. Jews could only become Swedes after being baptized, and the ceremonial drums of the Saami peoples were collected and destroyed. During the 20th century purity of race in Sweden became more important, and at some universities there was opposition to German Jewish doctors, who were being hunted by the Nazis, being granted asylum in Sweden.

This attitude changed completely – with the exception of a number of fanatics – during the second half of the 20th century, and as a symbol of the fact that stupidity can be replaced by diversity, one can now note the mosques where Muslims, who practice the second most common religion in Sweden, now congregate for prayer and Koran schools. Once upon a time there were German immigrants who gave Swedes celebrations such as May poles, bonfires on the eve of Walpurgis, Lucia, and Santa Claus or the *Jultomten*. After World War II, with a little help from mass media, the Anglo-Saxon holiday traditions appeared, including Halloween and Valentine's Day. How well will we accept the celebrations which today's immigrants have in their cultural baggage? Up until now they have had to accept the framework created by the Swedish calendar, however there are already a number of "exotic" holidays and celebrations that are now noted on our pocket calendars, although they have not yet been made red letter days.

Most ethnic Swedes do not know anything about the celebration cycles of their new neighbors, so the most important ones will be noted here in an effort to raise general awareness.

Islam

Islam's celebration calendar is based on the lunar year, and as most people know, it does not always synchronize with the solar year. A particular point in time which is determined by the moon moves eleven days every year. The first tradition on the Muslim calendar that we Swedes were introduced to via mass media was Ramadan, the month of fasting, which was very much focused on in the press in 2005. At the same time retailers realized the sales potential offered by *Eid-ul-fitr*, the major three day celebration at the end of Ramadan. Now a few years later, the Muslim festivities which usually are celebrated with an abundance of delicious foods, are an asset with a turnover in the billions which will soon be able to compete with our western Christmas trade. Ramadan is considered to be the holiest month by Muslims, and it is celebrated in memory of the prophet Muhammad receiving the revelations from God which were to become the Koran, the Muslim version of our Christian Bible. During Ramadan orthodox Muslims cannot eat, drink or smoke between sunrise and sunset, nor can they partake in lovemaking. However these rules make exceptions for children, sick people and old people, and there are special rules for what to do when traveling.

The other major Muslim celebration is *Id-al-Adha*, a sacrificial celebration that is held in memory of Abraham's willingness to offer his son, who through divine intervention later was replaced on the sacrificial altar by a lamb. Completely logical since the main dish served during the celebration is actually roast lamb.

Judaism

Even the Jewish calendar is based on the lunar year having twelve months of either 29 or 30 days. They have a system involving additional months since it was important that the major celebrations should fall at about the same time during the solar year.

Passover, the feast of the unleavened bread, is celebrated in memory of the flight from Egypt which happened so quickly that the dough did not have time to rise before everyone had to leave. The Pascal lamb had been slaughtered and eaten the day before and its blood had been used to mark the doorways so that the angel of death would hasten past the Jewish homes (the word Passover comes from the verb *Pesach* which means to pass by). Christianity inherited this Jewish celebration because the only sure date in the life of Jesus is his death during the Jewish Passover celebration, and this is the reason why the date of our Easter holiday changes according to the full moon, pretty much the way it did during the time of Jesus – a strange anomaly in the otherwise so regular annual course of our calendar.

The Feast of Weeks, *Shavuot*, is so called because it ends the seven week period after Passover. It falls on the fiftieth day, which the Greek Bible translators had in mind when they named this day Pentecost, based on *pentekoste*, the Greek word for fifty, which became the word *Pingst* in Swedish.

The autumn Sukkot Festival is an ancient harvest feast which is also associated with the flight from Egypt and the simple camps that were built then. It is celebrated for one week during the autumn month of Tishri.

Other Jewish celebrations of somewhat lesser "significance" are Hanukkah, the celebration of the re-dedication of the temple, and Purim which commemorates the memory of how Haman's plan to eradicate the Jews in Persia was foiled by the Jewish queen Esther. Both are markedly happy celebrations, particularly the weeklong celebration of Hanukkah, a festival of lights in the December darkness which is celebrated with a number of traditional dishes.

The Romani People

On April 8, 1971 the U. N. declared that the Romani, people who are also known as gypsies or *zigenare* in Swedish, were recognized as an ethnic minority. In Sweden they were not granted the same status until 1999. In most countries – Romanis are found almost everywhere in the world – April 8 was the day chosen to celebrate their National Day, and this happens in Sweden as well. There are many Romanis living here, approximately 8,000 people mostly in Malmö and environs where there is also a Romani cultural center.

The most well-known Romani festival is held May 24-25 in the village of Les-Saintes-Maries-de-la-Mer on the Mediterranean Camargue coast, where there is an ancient church built on top of a pre-Christian temple which houses a famous painting of Saint Sarah, Sara-Kali in Romani or Sara the Black. This village is named Maria in plural form because an old legend has it that several of the Marias in Jesus' family were forced into exile by the Jews and that they arrived on this coast together with a dark-skinned Egyptian servant named Sara. She performed miracles which led to a very apocryphal declaration of her sainthood. It is her portrait as a saint which great numbers of Romanis from many countries including Sweden travel here on pilgrimages to honor during a two day celebration. Sometimes she is given the title Mother of the Romanis, which historically makes as little sense as the name one can sometimes see, Queen of the Gypsies. However this does not cast a shadow upon the festival atmosphere in the entire village.

It was during the mid-19th century that the cult around Sara the Black reached its present proportions, with processions and sacrifices to the portrait of Sarah.